SWEDEN: THE MIDDLE WAY

SWEDEN

THE MIDDLE WAY

BY MARQUIS W. CHILDS

NEW HAVEN · YALE UNIVERSITY PRESS

TO

MY MOTHER

ACKNOWLEDGMENTS

Inadequate as this expression of gratitude necessarily is, I must thank Victor Proetz for my original interest in Sweden; Tage Palm for making my first visit to Scandinavia possible, and for a keen and continuing interest in this book from its inception, which has resulted in invaluable aid; Carl Milles for his warm hospitality in Stockholm; Per Wijkman for sage advice and counsel. Without the assistance of Naboth Hedin, who has made of the American-Swedish News Exchange an authentic medium of international understanding, I should not have been able to complete the book on this side of the Atlantic; I am deeply in his debt not only for the aid that was a part of his office as director of the Exchange in New York but for consideration and kindness far beyond that. Likewise Mr. Nils Horney, the Stockholm representative of the Exchange, gave me great help, simplifying my approach to Sweden. My wife has assisted me with the preparation of this book at every step and I can never thank her adequately nor express my appreciation of her keen critical sense and her constant devotion.

CONTENTS

ILLUSTRATIONS

(between pages 62 and 63)

All photographs courtesy of the American-Swedish News Exchange

Luma lightbulb factory. Owned and operated by the Swedish Coöperative Union and Wholesale Society.

Coöperative Tre Kronor (Three Crowns) flour mill, situated on island at the entrance to Stockholm's harbor.

Coöperative department store, Ljusdal.

Interior of coöperative supermarket, Stockholm.

"Elephant" (apartment) houses in suburban Hässelby Strand district, west of Stockholm.

Civic center of Vällingby, one of the new self-contained suburbs on the outskirts of Stockholm.

Slottsstadens coeducational high school in Malmö.

Public school in Vällingby being decorated by artists.

Worker's house at the Kosta Glassworks.

Old people's home, Sabbatsberg, Stockholm.

H. M. King Gustaf VI Adolf of Sweden.

Modern housing development in Stockholm.

The State Normal College in Stockholm. In the background: tower of the Stockholm stadium, built for the Olympic games in 1912.

Homes for workers at Gustavsberg coöperative ceramic factory.

INTRODUCTION TO THE
PAPERBOUND EDITION

I T is not easy today to appreciate the mood of the country when this book was first published twenty-five years ago. The New Deal had made a beginning. The blind, numb fear of three years before had been dispelled with the improvisation of hasty measures that thrust out in new directions everywhere. But there were still 10,000,000 persons or more seeking work and unable to find it. While they were no longer starving, plainly they could not exist indefinitely on the relief rolls or by the made work that had already come to be scornfully referred to as leaf-raking.

Would the choice in America finally come down to Communism or Fascism? As these two violent extremes became more and more openly embraced in Europe, there were many here who thought so. The Communists were exploiting the misery of the depression to the utmost. Their more naïve American disciples believed that the revolution was bound to come in what, in their interpretation, was an almost total breakdown of the capitalist system. Demagogues on the right, such as Huey Long, were likewise trying to exploit the discontent and distrust that were widespread in the growing disillusion with the early phase of the New Deal and its failure to "cure" mass unemployment.

Visiting Sweden in 1930 and again in 1933, I was deeply impressed by the way in which social and economic tools had been used to minimize the effect of the world-wide depression and to maintain a comparatively high standard of living. Above all, the approach seemed to me pragmatic and practical: divorced from the deadly dogmas that threatened to tear the world apart in a new kind of holy war. Having lived so long as a near neighbor of the Russians, engaging them in the

eighteenth and nineteenth centuries in one conflict after another, the Swedes understood that not a little of what was
happening in the Soviet Union was Russian, rather than Communist. The debt was to Peter the Great and the outward
thrust of czarist imperialism at least as much as it was to Karl
Marx.

What the Swedes were doing—in the coöperative movement,
in welfare measures such as unemployment insurance and
pensions, in public housing to erase the slums—was not new.
What seemed to me important and new was their objective in
employing these measures. The goal was not to make over
society by some foreordained prescription. It was to modify
and moderate, and thereby make more workable the system
already in being. One goal, certainly of the leading coöperators,
was to curb the excesses of capitalism—to check the rise of
monopolies that imposed high prices. While the Social-Democratic party, already the dominant political party, had a core
of socialist doctrine, this gradually lost its significance for most
members of the party. And while the left-of-center parties
inveighed in parliamentary debate at times against the institution of royalty, the unifying presence of the King was generally
valued by all classes. I tried to say that while this was a small
country with a homogeneous population smaller than that of
the city of New York, its achievements might nevertheless be
relevant to the dilemma in which the United States found itself.

No one could have been more surprised than I, unless perhaps
it was the publisher, by the book's reception. Almost without
exception the reviewers acclaimed it. In early 1936, conservatives in the Democratic party had begun to turn against
Franklin Roosevelt and his New Deal. Alfred E. Smith had
said that he was going to take a walk. Lewis Gannett, then the
daily reviewer for the *New York Herald-Tribune,* advised
Smith to take his walk in Sweden. Noting this suggestion,
John Chamberlain, reviewing for the *New York Times,* wrote:

> The advice is good. But the thought occurs to one who
> can see no real socialism whatever in the New Deal (it

looks to me like a dodge to save the shirts of the very Liberty Leaguers who are denouncing it day and night) that Franklin D. Roosevelt also ought to take a walk in Sweden. For Sweden's "middle way" between economic individualism and collectivism is designed to expand production and to lower costs and prices, whereas the New Deal "socialism" works in the opposite direction. The American New Deal is an experiment in the "socialization of losses," and it tends to push capitalism just so much further along the road to monopoly, with all its evils.

The book became an immediate best seller and the publisher was startled to discover one edition after another sold almost before it was off the presses. Thanks to syndication, excerpts were published in newspapers across the country. The *New York Daily News* devoted a full column editorial to "the middle way," calling the book "almost indispensable" to an understanding of how controls could be applied to capitalism without wrecking the machine. Although he put more stress on the socialist nature of the labor movement in Sweden, Norman Thomas, in *The Nation,* gave it a magisterial nod of approval. In the summer, Roosevelt named a commission to go to Europe and study the coöperative movement in England and Scandinavia.

The word "utopia" recurred in the reviews and in the extended discussion of the book by leading public figures with embarrassing frequency. While I had been enthusiastic about Sweden, its people, and the experiments they were undertaking, I had not meant to convey an impression of utopia. On the contrary, I had been interested because this was not an effort to impose a prefabricated utopia. Nor had I thought of it as a "pattern" that other far larger and more diverse nations might follow. The lessons were there and they could be applied, it seemed to me, but only with a realization of the limitations of the example.

Looking back, I see now that I failed to stress sufficiently the discipline imposed on a people who must make the utmost use of their resources in order to send their finished goods into the stream of world trade. This has served as a brake on almost every element in the country. Thus it was possible to agree on a system of compulsory arbitration which virtually eliminated both strikes and lockouts. Wage demands and price increases have to some degree been restrained by the need to compete in the world market.

While I emphasized the importance of the fact that Sweden had been at peace since the end of the Napoleonic Wars early in the nineteenth century, it would be hard to exaggerate this factor. One has only to look at the budgets of the great powers to see the extent to which the cost of past wars in veterans' care, pensions, interest on the debt, and in other less obvious ways, makes it difficult to find revenue for current pressing needs. Although the great wars have taken their toll, and in some respects a heavy one, the peace has been kept for nearly 150 years. To be able to subtract from the American budget the cost of the Civil War, the Spanish-American War, the two world wars, and the Korean War is to get an idea of the margin that Sweden has enjoyed in social planning and development.

But when due allowances are made for the accident of geography and the good fortune of history, the organizing ability of the Swedes is seen to be of a very high order. The sustained capacity for organization is evident in both the public and the private sector. On the latter, I put insufficient stress if only because I was trying to show how Sweden differed from other highly organized capitalist societies. Swedish industry is as advanced in technology and science as any in the world. That a nation of seven and a half million people can manufacture automobiles for export and jet planes to equip seven of the eight wings of the Swedish air force is one indication of the capacity of industry to compete with far larger and, in many ways, richer countries.

The reaction in Sweden to the book's extraordinary reception in America, the rush, as it were, to discover a new utopia, was revealing. Bankers and industrialists complained that I had exaggerated the part played in the economy by the public and coöperative sector. In doing this I had ignored, or at any rate denigrated, the role of private enterprise which was central to the success Sweden had enjoyed. But perhaps more significant was a concern that I had painted in far too glowing colors the good fortune that the country happened to be enjoying. There came into play here a curious facet of the Swedish character; an almost superstitious fear of advertising good fortune. You are certain, if you rise too high, to be the object of envy and distrust and this can have only unhappy consequences. The Swedes foresaw that their "middle way" would attract critics determined to explode the whole concept and expose it, insofar as it might be based on welfare measures, as a fraud.

Just this has happened. Writers, editors, economists have never ceased to pass judgment. The tendency of many critics has been to ascribe every flaw in the nation's life to the unnatural security created by the cradle-to-grave welfare measures Sweden has adopted. The suicide rate, the increase in drunkenness, juvenile delinquency, children's neglect of their aging parents, all the sins of omission and commission are put down to the paternalism of the state. One of the most remarkable manifestations of this phenomenon was seen in President Eisenhower's remarks to Republicans during the national convention in Chicago in the summer of 1960. On the basis of information that had apparently come to him at second or third hand, he intimated, without actually naming the country, that Sweden's "socialism" had increased the rate of drunkenness and suicide and was producing a nation of wastrels.

In this is a kind of economic determinism rivaling the dogmas of Marxism. It blandly ignores so much that is relevant to the particular social structure—the kind of society—that Sweden has evolved. Take, as an example, the century and a half of peace. In an earlier era the Swedish character was conditioned by a series of terrible wars, by conflict, suffering, hunger, loss of life and limb. One may well ask how such a prolonged season of peace affects the human psyche. Is the challenge of war essential to the vigor and vitality of the human spirit? William James wrote of the imperative need to find a "moral equivalent of war" that would bring out the bravest and best in human conduct. No very marked progress has been made in this direction, either in Sweden or anywhere else.

Hitler invaded Norway and Denmark in 1940 at the same time that he launched his invasion of the Low Countries and France. Sweden was left alone to try to steer a course of precarious neutrality—a course that was compromised by the fact that German troops crossed the country at regular intervals going to and from occupied Norway. Swedish iron from the rich deposits in the north went down to Hitler Germany. Knowing how their closest neighbors and next of kin were suffering under the occupation, the Swedes were sorely troubled. They consoled themselves with the belief that in providing an escape hatch through which the underground could operate, they were doing more than they possibly could if they sacrificed themselves in a gesture of defiance toward the Nazis. But who can say what a strain on the conscience it must have been to have come through the war still relatively prosperous and untouched.

The ills that go with ever-increasing urbanism have afflicted the Swedes as they have other larger and more diverse societies. The trend has been to small apartments that help to fragment the family unit and remove the center of interest outside the home. In Sweden it is believed to have contributed to the stationary or declining birth rate. To some degree welfare measures, such as public housing on a large scale and efforts to check the rise of land values, have mitigated the ills that accompany the growing concentration of life in cities such as Stockholm or Gothenburg. Nevertheless, no one would be foolish enough to assume that a so-called welfare state, however perfectly constituted, would be a warranty against the evils that have everywhere accompanied industrialization and city living.

For nearly thirty years Sweden has been governed by the same party, the Social-Democrats. They have been in coalition at times with the Farmers' party, but essentially the same men with the same ideas have prevailed. Neither the Conservatives nor the Liberals have offered the electorate a sufficiently appealing alternative. However one may explain this—and the Conservatives would put it down to the higher pensions, the complete medical care, and other benefits offered by the labor party—few would argue that it is a desirable situation. It suggests the managerial society in which ideas have been made subordinate to the adjustment of welfare measures to mass necessity.

But again, Sweden is not unique in this respect. In England it is difficult, if not impossible, to see an alternative to the Tories, who have so cleverly appropriated the whole range of Labor Party palliatives while at the same time exorcising the devil of doctrinaire socialism. In our own country the Democrats were in power for twenty years when Republican fortune in annexing a hero-general broke the sequence for eight years.

The organizing capacity of the Swedes seems to be unimpaired. The current statistics—and Swedish statistics are as reliable as those of any in the world—tell at least the superficial aspects of the story. In life expectancy, Sweden stands third among the nations, with only Norway and the Netherlands having a better record. In infant mortality, Sweden is first with the lowest number of infant deaths. This says something about Sweden's high standards of medical knowledge and research, and also perhaps about the system of "socialized" medicine which has been so roundly condemned. This book does not include a discussion of that system, which could well be the subject of a separate and full-length exposition. Incidentally, the individual is given free choice of the kind of medical care he prefers, which one would not infer from the numerous critics.

By commonly accepted indicators of prosperity, the Swedes are flourishing. There are 1,200,000 cars in operation, which means on the average a car for every five to six persons. The number of telephones is above 2,500,000. The number of television sets licensed was more than one million in 1960, and by the end of 1961 it is expected that there will be on the average one set for every family.

In 1959, when the new old-age pension plan was adopted, Prime Minister Tage Erlander said that it was the last major piece of welfare legislation. A system financed by employers, it provides a pension after 67 of two-thirds of the individual's average earnings during his or her best fifteen years. The Conservatives and the Liberals bitterly fought it. In fact, the measure was adopted thanks to the defection of one Liberal member of parliament, who was then disciplined by expulsion, although later the party adopted the pension plan as part of its program.

During the booming fifties there was overemployment. One unhappy result about which many Swedes complained was the falling off of all services. The government's problem was to bring in workers from abroad to try to meet the need. More recently unemployment has stood at about four per cent, which is generally considered the equivalent of full employment. The price level has risen as it has elsewhere, and part of the government's effort, far from successful, has been to hold prices down. In 1959, the wholesale price index was 144, with 1949 at 100; and the level in 1949 was at 216 using 100 in 1935 as the base. The gross national product, allowing for the changes in computation growing out of the fiscal reforms, roughly doubled between 1946 and 1959.

Does all this mean that Sweden has solved her problems, and that the Swedes are a happy and contented people? Of course it does not, and only an economic determinist could assume that it would or should. In part, the familiar ills of advancing industrialization—the technological revolution— have been ameliorated. But the suicide rate does remain high; it has always been high in Sweden and Denmark, with the long, dark winters regarded as a possible contributory factor. The rate of drunkenness, which went up with the abolition of the Bratt system of liquor control, has begun to go down again. In the nuclear age the Swedes suffer from living on the brink of annihilation, as does the rest of the world. Although, it may be added, nothing could illustrate better the combination of accident and organizing capacity which has resulted in Sweden being the only country really ready to protect its population from nuclear attack. The accident was the granite formation on which Stockholm is built and which made possible the construction of deep shelters at a much lower cost than they could be constructed elsewhere. The "middle way" is still an experiment that may have something to say to far more diverse societies with more difficult and complicated problems. Sweden is not utopia and, given the norms of human nature, the stubborn persistence of human discontent, jealousy, frustration, and malice, it never will be.

M.W.C.

Washington, D.C.
March 1961

SWEDEN : THE MIDDLE WAY

I

THE BEGINNING OF COÖPERATION

COÖPERATION was an established movement with an extensive development not only in England, where it originated, but on the continent as well, long before it found a place in Sweden. In its origins in England it had Utopian overtones. To the earnest weavers of Rochdale, with their new coöperative society, it seemed that the profit motive must be transformed and society remade through the force of their idea. Their interest in the philosophical implications of the movement seems to have been fully as great as their immediate concern over the practical benefits which they might derive.

The approach to coöperation in Sweden, with the exception of certain early and futile experiments, was different. The Swedes were primarily interested from the beginning in lower prices and higher quality, to be obtained through distribution and, later, production for use instead of profit.

Early coöperatives in England had failed because they had tried, while still weak and struggling, to undersell their private competitors. In contrast, the Rochdale movement was founded on the policy of selling at the market, the doctrines of classical economics. This was the reason for the first success of the Rochdale coöperatives, but with increasing monopoly, which more and more invalidated the "laws" of supply and demand, British coöperators found themselves in the profit-making class.

In its inception the coöperative movement in Sweden was patterned after the Rochdale model. But an early aim of Swedish coöperative leaders was to destroy monopoly. As they gathered strength, they dared to fix their own prices at whatever level they considered reasonable. This, it will be seen, is an important distinction.

In its external forms, too, Sweden followed the English coöperative plan. Individual societies, most of them at the outset in towns and cities, and especially in industrial areas, enrolled members who each subscribed a fixed amount of share capital in order to establish the retail store of the society. These struggling societies finally united, in 1899, to form the Kooperativa Förbundet (The Coöperative Union), known familiarly the length and breadth of the land as K.F. It combined the functions of both the Coöperative Wholesale Society and the Coöperative Union in England, and its formation was the beginning of the rapid development of the coöperative movement.

The coöperative idea attracted at this time certain young men who soon demonstrated that they possessed not alone zeal for the cause but a high degree of business acumen. These men, among them Anders Örne, Ernst Persson, Axel Gjöres, and above all Albin Johansson, have had not a little to do with the extraordinary rise of K.F. In fact business apologists are inclined to attribute the success of the movement entirely to the shrewdness of a few leaders such as Johansson. But it was more than ordinary business shrewdness which they brought to their first difficult task.

The first organizers were compelled to pay their own traveling expenses. And growth must have seemed dishearteningly slow. By 1904 the wholesale turnover of K.F. was about $75,000 which, small as it was, permitted employment of a full-time manager to direct the wholesale trade of the Union at headquarters in Stockholm, the leading city as well as the capital. The work of organization was being pushed forward, and slowly the Swedes, particularly the industrial workers in the towns, grasped the practical meaning of coöperation.

Swedish coöperators sought from the outset to keep their stores free from the institutional character they had assumed elsewhere. The stores were open to the trade of the public and although nonmembers did not receive the annual dividend—in effect a rebate on the year's purchases—they might allow this dividend to accumulate toward the cost of the initial membership shares. Small and limited as the stores were in the early years, it was not long before private trade began to recognize the implications of this new form of competition and to act in self-preservation.

Retail merchants first succeeded, by a threat of boycott, in forcing wholesalers to refuse any further business with K.F. The only immediate result of this was that the Coöperative Union, which had up to this time traded solely as an agency, now began timidly to buy abroad and at home on its own initiative, establishing its own warehouse at Malmö, the third largest city in Sweden, situated on the southernmost tip of the peninsula. With this the retailers, who had formed a "protective" association, carried the battle one step further. They enlisted the aid of powerful cartels which dominated the domestic supply of certain necessities. These local cartels were in certain instances merely units of larger trusts that dominated European trade.

Among the most powerful of the local cartels was the one that dominated the trade in margarine. The thrifty Scandinavians export much of their butter fat to England and to the continent and margarine is therefore a staple need. The wholesale department of the Union was just getting established on a relatively sound basis, but it could not ignore this challenge. For it was quite plain that the question would be ultimately one of survival. The Union entered the fight boldly, amassing all its resources to buy a small margarine factory that was not within the control of the cartel.

For the struggling young Union the price war that followed was perhaps the most fortunate thing that could have occurred at this time although it did not so appear at the moment. It was a perfect demonstration, which the Union was quick to point out in its propaganda, of monopoly control over prices. The public was well aware that the margarine cartel had considered changing the price of margarine at the beginning of 1909, reaching a final decision that no reduction was possible. But with the announcement that the Union had bought a factory and was preparing to manufacture margarine, the cartel quickly lowered its price. The Union in its advertisements made it plain to consumers that this had been done despite the fact that there had been no change in the cost of raw materials, and that the public was under obligations to K.F. for the lowered price.

The total capital of the Union, including reserves, was less than $35,000 and with its existence at stake it now appealed to the public for support. The first step was to offer for sale bonds of less than $3 each, repayable in ten years at 50 per cent above their cost. Within a brief time $15,000 was subscribed and this sum would have been greatly increased if it had not been for the action of the public prosecutor who intervened at the insistence of a newspaper bitterly hostile to the coöperative movement. The technicality raised against the sale of the bonds—that they should have carried a stamp duty—was rejected by the supreme court, but long after the Union had been forced to withdraw unsold bonds from the market.

It may be noted, in passing, that Swedish law is comparatively direct and simple, and is codified in a single volume. That volume and the Bible are to be found in most Swedish homes even when there are no other books. The Swedish farmer can take down his law book, turn to page and subject, and read the law for himself. Precedent plays but a small part in the decisions of the courts, which is doubtless why the law is a limited profession in Sweden.

For two years longer the struggle continued. In 1911 the margarine cartel was broken up and prices went to a level which the coöperators considered justifiable from the point of view of cost of manufacture and distribution. It had been a complete victory for K.F. The public was given this tangible proof of the power of coöperation, a lesson which the coöperators were not slow to drive home, and as for the coöperative societies, they were united as never before. With this victory in the background, the Union with renewed confidence carried the price war to other fronts, combating monopolies in sugar, soap, chocolate, flour, rubber.

These contests—and the outcome in each instance was like the outcome of the margarine war—all show the remarkable ability of the Swedes to concentrate upon an immediate, practical problem, bringing to the issue of the price of potatoes not only intelligence and acumen but even a kind of ardor. When the historian of coöperation in Sweden speaks of the nation watching with "rapt attention" the course of these struggles it is more than a figure of speech.

The leaders of the coöperative movement were of the firm conviction that only consumers themselves, banded together in their own self-interest, could curb the greed of monopoly. It was a time when world attention was focused upon the power of the trusts. There was a slow realization that capitalism was passing into a monopoly phase; that industry and wealth were being concentrated at a more and more rapid rate in an ever narrower circle. In America the first President Roosevelt was urging the passage of laws to "bust the trusts" and protect the "little man." In Sweden those who have been most active in the warfare against monopoly control of wealth and industry have never at any time relied upon the law; legal barriers against monopoly are entirely futile in the opinion of these practical leaders. Thus the directors of the coöperative movement carried on the fight against the trusts, directly on the firing line in wholesale and retail trade, not only for the practical advantage of the Coöperative Union but as a fundamental social duty.

On several new fronts the war on the trusts went forward. One of the most predatory of all the cartels was that controlling the flour-milling industry. Formed in 1914, it ruled with unrelenting watchfulness over the entire industry, providing heavy penalties for violation of price stipulations and fixed milling quotas and working through an agreement with the wholesalers to prevent the importation of flour from abroad except in very limited quantities. This monopoly was so comprehensive that no individual miller would have dared to defy it. While before the formation of the cartel the mills had paid a stock profit that averaged from 8 to 9 per cent, in the first year after the trust was formed profits increased to 23 per cent and for at least one year they were even higher, reaching, in 1919, 33 per cent, partly the result of wartime inflation.

Year after year parliament and the press stormed and scolded at this cartel. It was blasted and lampooned by politicians and editorial writers, but to no avail whatsoever. In the fall of 1922, through a shrewd piece of strategy, the Coöperative Union was able to buy, at a price that was not too unreasonable, one of the largest mills in the country, Tre Kronor (Three Crowns), at the entrance to Stockholm harbor. As a first step the mill, and it is a large one judged from any standard, was remodeled from top to bottom so that when it was ready for operation in 1924 it was the most efficient mill in Sweden. Then began the struggle which the whole country watched with "rapt attention."

K.F. demonstrated that, thanks in part to a large body of loyal coöperators, it could stand up to a rival with the power of the milling cartel. When the cartel cut prices below the cost of production, K.F. and its affiliated retail societies stood fast, knowing that even the trust could not long continue this ruinous practice and that in the interval the coöperatives would have the assured trade of their faithful membership. Through skilful propaganda it was possible to make clear the significance of this battle and there was little wavering from the coöperative line. Victory was made certain when K.F. managed to buy a second large mill, Tre Lejon (Three Lions), at Gothenburg, the second city of Sweden. Less than two years after K.F. began to manufacture flour, the cartel was painfully attempting to adjust its prices to coöperative prices and never quite succeeding, for the coöperative price remained from twelve to twenty-five cents a sack below the trust price.

The stern necessities created by the World War in almost every Swedish household had given the coöperative movement a tremendous impetus. Although membership in the early years grew slowly and it was not until 1913 that the hundred thousand mark was passed, this number was doubled in four years and trebled in the decade after 1913. By 1925 the coöperatives could claim, on a basis of the most conservative estimates, about 20 per cent of the population. In the more prosperous midlands this proportion was much higher. While Swedish coöperators were well aware that this ratio was lower than in other countries, particularly low in comparison to Scotland and England, they held to the view that they had brought about, by following the line of true coöperation—of distribution and production for use—greater benefits to the consuming public as a whole. And to substantiate this view they had the report of a Swedish Government Commission appointed in 1922 to investigate the middleman's profit. The commission said:

It is clear that consumers' coöperation offers a vigorous defense against the tendencies of private trade to combine in order to keep up prices artificially. Many examples could be mentioned where large organizations of shopkeepers have been forced by the coöperative society to scale down their prices—an act which the trade associations by themselves otherwise would have prevented. The great importance of the coöperative movement in this respect has been proved in a remarkable degree, particularly during the period of declining values, when the coöperative societies, as a rule, have been the first to reduce prices.

Coöperation developed with a curious classlessness in which the coöperators themselves took a certain pride. Well aware that the mass of industrial workers formed the core of the movement, they took it as a symbol of the universal value of coöperation that a prince of the blood royal should be a member of the Stockholm Coöperative Society and that during the war this society had as its chairman a cabinet minister, Baron Palmstjerna, a member of an old and distinguished family. It was not that the upper class condescended to encourage the movement. In part they had been responsible for starting it.

In the early phase one of the strongest groups had been the society in Stockholm known as Swedish Homes, founded and directed, to use Axel Gjöres' phrase, "by middle and upper class ladies." This society opened its first store in 1905, to be met with a boycott prepared in advance by apprehensive merchants of the capital. But Swedish Homes, having a considerable reserve to draw upon, was able to finance the purchase of supplies from coöperative wholesales in Holland and England and thereby defeat the boycott. Later Swedish Homes merged with K.F.S., the Stockholm Coöperative Society, which has not only the largest but also the most aggressive membership of any of the local societies.

Among small land owners and farmers the movement was very slow to take root. After the war, however, the largest rate of increase was in rural areas, a development which was extremely gratifying to the leaders of the movement; between 1913 and 1925 the number of farm members grew from 11,000 to 43,000. In the latter year the membership of societies affiliated to K.F. was divided as follows:

	Per cent of total
Farmers and small land owners	15.2
Farm workers	4.7
Small workshop masters	3.1
Small workshop workers	5.2
Professional, civil service	2.4
Clerks, public employees	8.2
Industrial and factory workers .	29.3
Other workers	20.5
Corporations	1.0
Others	10.4

In general this is said to approximate the proportions to be found in the population. "This development," one of the co-operative leaders adds, "is the more gratifying in that there has not been the slightest sign of any ill-will between the various groups, but all have put aside their class or political interests and have united in common labor on the problems cooperation aims to solve."

As the scope, both of the Coöperative Union (the manufacturer and wholesaler) and the local societies (the retail distributing outlets) grew under the impetus of the war and the post-war inflation, great care was taken to preserve democratic control. With the realism that characterizes their political thinking, the Swedes foresaw that in a society numbering thousands of members the old form, under which a member was required to attend a general meeting in order to participate in the affairs of the society, would permit control by an aggressive minority. The Stockholm Society, confronted with this problem, undertook a series of experiments which resulted in the creation of new forms whereby the function of self-government might be assured to the whole membership.

The area served by the Stockholm Society was divided into eighteen districts. At a meeting held prior to the General Meeting each district elects representatives, one for every 300 members. At the General Meeting, made up of these elected delegates, to the number of 300, each representative has one vote. Here all questions affecting the membership as a whole are decided; what to do with the trading surplus, the "profit"; important problems of policy raised at district meetings; whether to approve or disapprove the management report. Within the province of the district meeting, of course, are details of management in that particular district. But to prevent the diffusion, the quibbling over minor points of shop conduct which would inevitably result, each district names a members' council or district committee of from three to five members. This committee must make a comprehensive report on shop conduct at the district meeting and in discussion of the committee's report the members have full opportunity to advance criticisms, suggestions, proposed changes and innovations. Thus any member may in the proper order protest the price of herring or a shop clerk's inefficiency.

This system went far toward solving the relationship of the society to its membership. But there remained the problem of business management. As the coöperatives extended their activities to new and more complex fields, it was apparent that for day-to-day efficiency authority must be delegated to an executive empowered to make the decisions that a business of any size constantly requires. The Stockholm Society created a board of directors composed of the three heads of the main departments of the society, grocery, bakery, and office. It is scarcely necessary to add that these three paid executives hold their positions by virtue of their demonstrated capacities. This executive board was given the right of decision "in all business questions of recurrent character and in financial questions of minor importance, and in the employment and dismissal of staff, in accordance, of course, with agreements in force."

Ultimate authority over matters involving larger sums or issues of principle are referred to a management council composed of fifteen members elected at the General Meeting of the society. The executives themselves are appointed to their positions by this council. The council meets once a month to consider and decide questions referred to it by the executive board under rules and instructions carefully drawn up. The three members of the executive board are required to attend this meeting, submit a report and supply any details not contained in that report.

It might seem at first glance that this machinery of government would be unwieldy by its very emphasis upon democracy. But it has functioned efficiently. The reason may be that Swedish coöperators have taken a serious and sustained interest in the business of their district, of their society, and of the Union to which their society belongs. There have been complaints of indifference, of course, but always there has been a large and active majority willing to give time and thought to the business of the group. The men at the top, at the head of the Coöperative Union are, as has been said, exceptionally keen business men, but nevertheless, if the interest of the coöperators themselves should lag, I believe there would be a heavy loss in efficiency throughout the whole system.

K.F., the Coöperative Union, is organized in much the same way as are the larger retail societies. Unlike the British Coöperative Union, which embraces a number of units that each carry on different functions, K.F. itself is wholesaler, manufacturer, educator, and propagandist. This kind of central organization, which is found elsewhere only in Denmark, Norway, and Switzerland, has worked to the advantage of Swedish coöperators.

It was in 1918 that the parliamentary machinery of K.F. was recast, following closely the model of the Stockholm Society, with a management council charged with final responsibility at the top. This council of eighteen members, elected at meetings of the thirteen districts into which the country is divided, is split up into various subcommittees, each responsible for the supervision of a particular department. Although the council, which must elect the paid executives of K.F., is required to meet only four times a year, in practice it meets much oftener. Besides the duty of supervision, the council must make important decisions as to new ventures; the purchase and sale of property; the investment of surplus capital; and the adjustment of collective agreements with employees.

As with the larger retail societies, there is an executive board made up of the heads of the principal departments, with the paid president in the office of managing director over the entire business. Under this general plan, the annual Congress of the whole society is left free to shape general policy through debate and discussion, with the duty of passing upon the report of the management council and electing auditors. The latter are, in a sense, a separate entity, detached from the rest of the organization in order to insure absolute impartiality in their audit.

One reason for the practical success of coöperation has been the program of education intended to help the paid employees of the retail societies to advance themselves, and incidentally, of course, improve the service in the stores. K.F. has an Educational Department that directs a number of branches of study, both by correspondence and in special classes and schools. The correspondence courses have been particularly successful, enrolling many outside the coöperative movement for study in such practical subjects as bookkeeping, arithmetic, commercial correspondence, mercantile law and banking, and even more rudimentary essentials such as grammar and composition.

Employees who show rapid progress are given every encouragement and offered further education to make advancement to a higher post possible. There is a free class lasting for four weeks to prepare the most advanced clerks to become branch managers, and having covered the required work in this field, they may attend still another class leading to a higher position. Besides these classes there are summer schools for store managers.

And propaganda is by no means neglected. The principal coöperative publication, the weekly *Vi,* distributed through the retail stores, has the largest circulation of any periodical or paper in the country. It is an attractive, smart looking magazine that would compare favorably with the best popular journals anywhere. The reverse of highbrow, it publishes serially the novels of the most popular writers in the country and seasons its propaganda with amusing articles and stories.

The fact that the coöperative movement has concentrated on practical achievements, with little consideration for the ultimate aim of rebuilding society, often distresses the more conscientious coöperators. They are somewhat apologetic for the fact that foreigners find the annual congress of the Union dull and boring, taken up with the price of knäckebröd and the development of the newest margarine factory, lacking in fine flights of oratory.

The Swede apparently has a curious resistance to abstract arguments. An account that appeared in *Vi* several years ago illustrates this very well. At Mellerud, a town of 1,500 inhabitants in the southwest of Sweden, a lecturer employed by the merchants' association gave a talk against the coöperatives. At the end of his talk there was lively discussion and the crowd, unwilling to disperse when the lights in the public hall were turned out, adjourned to another meeting place. There the argument continued into the early morning and finally closed with the unanimous adoption of a resolution that said: "We the undersigned 175 consumers here assembled in Mellerud tender our sincere thanks to Lecturer Lien for his anti-coöperative address, which has so completely persuaded us that we decide here and now to form ourselves into a coöperative society."

With a well-integrated, rapidly growing organization, Swedish coöperators were ready to go forward to new triumphs—over galoshes this time. It sounds funny but it is not at all; the victory over the galosh cartel—really the rubber cartel—was a very tangible achievement. Galoshes are a necessity in the Swedish winter, to say nothing of the Swedish spring and the Swedish fall. And four manufacturing firms, formed into an air-tight cartel, exploited this necessity for years. Annual profits of 60 per cent, 62 per cent and even, in one exceptional year, 77 per cent were recorded. On a capital of less than a million dollars the four factories realized in fourteen years more than twelve and a half million dollars and voted many stock dividends besides. As in the case of the milling cartel, the public yelled long and loud but with no visible results.

At the annual coöperative congress in 1926 it was decided that K.F. should declare war on the galosh cartel. This was the unanimous and enthusiastic opinion of the Congress. Within a few weeks, merely on the basis of this announcement, the cartel reduced the price of a pair of men's galoshes more than fifty cents, with corresponding reductions all down the line. K.F. informed the cartel that this was not enough, and when there were no further reductions the war was begun in earnest.

The cartel was obviously not going to sell one of its factories at anything like a reasonable price but when K.F. threatened to build a plant of its own, the enemy heeded the warning, recalling what had happened to other cartels that had remained adamant. In a remarkably short time K.F. had negotiated the purchase of a factory at Gislaved, and by January 1, 1927, after complete modernization, it took over operation of this plant. The result, within a year, was another seventy cents sliced off the price of a pair of galoshes. Having achieved this, K.F. began the manufacture of automobile tires at the Gislaved plant and by 1932 was producing 50,000 tires a year.

This then is what Swedish coöperation has set out to do. It is very little concerned with short cuts to Utopia. Interest and energy and will are concentrated on the cost of bread and galoshes and housing and automobile tires and insurance and electricity, all the "necessities" that go to make up a high standard of living. It has expanded from year to year until today the good coöperator in Sweden may live and die within his own system, a system based upon production for use rather than for profit.

II

WHAT THE COÖPERATIVES HAVE ACHIEVED

PRACTICAL shopkeepers that they are, the Swedish coöperators have taken the greatest care to present their wares in the most attractive form. Even in a land where the shape of the commonest things has a distinction, it is not difficult to pick out the coöperative shops. They are functional in that they have been designed to serve a definite purpose in the most efficient manner, but coöperative architecture has not been bound by an arbitrary formula. Simplicity, precision of line and a forthright honesty in the handling of materials give the coöp. stores a smartness, even a kind of beauty, that sets them apart in whatever neighborhood they may be.

Apples and oranges, eggs and potatoes, scrubbed and polished and put in handsome containers, all contribute to the design of the interior. The covering on the floor, a kind of linoleum, is in broad bands of contrasting color. The packages on the shelves seem to have been arranged with a sense of harmonious design rather than with any more practical end in view. The entire shop front is an unbroken expanse of plate glass and so the store is bright even on gray days when the winter sun hardly leaves the horizon.

There are 380 such shops in the Stockholm area alone, operated by the Stockholm consumers' society. The name KONSUM done in heavy block letters above the shop window immediately catches the eye. They are like the smart stores that one sees on the more expensive streets of an American city. But the several stores of the coöperative society of Kiruna, beyond the Arctic Circle, have the same distinctive appearance.

The Stockholm housewife comes to do her marketing here as she would in any private shop. She has read in her newspaper an advertisement listing the day's prices. This advertisement has appeared in all the morning newspapers and another will appear in the evening papers, covering special price changes—daily bargains—for all of the society's 380 shops; just as a private chain of grocery stores would advertise in the press of an American city. If the housewife, or any member of her household, is a member of the coöperative society, she presents her membership book to the clerk who enters in it the amount of her purchases, very much as an American shopper might save trading stamps toward a future bonus. On the total amount of purchases for the year the Stockholm household belonging to the coöperative society receives a dividend of 3 per cent.

The shopper who is not a member of the society in most instances effects an outright saving merely by coming to the coop. to do her marketing. For the coöperatives in recent years have been on the whole successful in keeping their price level below that of private retail stores. And once one has begun to buy at the coöp., there is a strong inducement to become a member of the society. Accounts are kept of dividends that accrue to nonmembers as scrupulously as for members; and by joining within a prescribed time limit, which is more than a year, the nonmember may apply his accumulated dividends to the purchase of the initial amount of share capital that all must own. If the nonmember fails to join within the prescribed time, his accumulated dividend is transferred to the society's reserve fund. Thus the members of the society in no way profit by sales to nonmembers, and the line of true coöperation is maintained. The rapid growth of the coöperatives in recent years is ascribed in part to this system of permitting—of encouraging— outsiders to sample coöperative wares and methods.

It is not a caste or a sect which the householder has joined. Unless she becomes an ardent and active coöperator, membership will mean little difference in her way of life; although, of course, if her household is run on a careful budget, she will doubtless observe a welcome surplus at the end of the year. There may be a study or social group in connection with the store with which she has become affiliated, but whether she takes any part in this activity will be a matter for her choice. Eventually she may be assigned to a committee with certain duties but these will not be difficult or burdensome unless she elects to make them so. To a large degree the type of membership and the activities in which people take part will depend on the neighborhood in which the new member lives.

In the upper middle class there exists a kind of scorn for the coöperatives, for the idea of economies so petty. But this attitude conceals in part a realization of what inroads coöperation has made upon private trade throughout the entire country. The Kreuger crash, however, did a great deal to liquidate this scorn. The households of many haughty army officers and over-confident speculators caught in the Kreuger catastrophe were suddenly grateful for the economies of coöperation. Recruits from the middle class, particularly in its upper reaches, may account for the steady growth of the coöperatives through the depression.

At the present time more than 10 per cent of the retail and wholesale trade of Sweden is carried on through the coöperatives. No satisfactory estimate can be made of the volume of manufacture done in coöperative factories; almost the entire volume, it should be added, being goods for domestic consumption. Statistics of production give only an approximate idea of the importance of coöperation in the commerce of the country. Well over a third of all the households in Sweden are enrolled in coöperative societies. This contrasts with England where more than 45 per cent of all households have one or more co-operative memberships and with Scotland where the coöperative membership includes nearly 55 per cent of all families. But Swedish coöperators suggest that they have succeeded in bringing about more profound changes with respect to the general price level—that is, to the benefit of the entire population—than has coöperation in Great Britain.

The depression has proved beyond reasonable doubt the stability of the coöperative movement. The books of the Union show gains in every department. The only decline has been in the number of societies and that has been the result of a deliberate policy of merging small societies to form larger and stronger units. In 1926 there were 846 societies with 339,273 families holding membership. In 1931 the number of societies was 697 with 481,319 family memberships; in 1932, 675 societies had 512,968 members; in 1934, it was 635 and 550,615;

and by 1936 the number of societies was 633 with a membership of 585,290. The number of stores owned by local societies was 2,411 in 1926, 3,510 in 1931, 3,716 in 1932, 3,868 in 1933, and 3,990 for 1934. And the annual turnover rose correspondingly, from 265,073,000 kronor in 1926, to 347,981,000 in 1931, 350,765,000 in 1932, 350,992,000 in 1933, and 376,373,-800 for 1934, with marked increases in each of the three years that have followed, the curve mounting slowly but steadily upward in the decade from 1926 to 1936.

The directors of the Coöperative Union were foresighted enough to see the economic storm of 1929 approaching. They faced the inevitability of a world-wide depression as early as 1931. From that time onward the economy of the local societies was directed along the most conservative lines. By 1932 the financial position of the Union and its affiliated societies was stronger than ever before. Trade debts had been reduced on the joint balance sheet from 38 per cent to less than 6 per cent and, not satisfied with this, the directors pushed toward the goal of buying, as the societies sell, for cash only.

The powerful parent organization may well be the principal reason for the success of the coöperative movement. The Union is owned by the 635 member societies, the proportion of ownership being based on the amount of capital contributed to the central organization, the number of members enrolled and the volume of annual sales. In actual practice it is more nearly as though K.F. owned the retail stores. However it is not a question of ownership. The retail societies could hardly exist without the Union, and the latter would have no function without store outlets.

K.F. performs innumerable services for the societies affiliated to it. A permanent staff of architects is constantly working to improve store plans, and their achievements in the direction of efficiency have been widely imitated in Europe. Local societies may obtain from K.F. standard designs for stores of varying size. The Union will give active assistance in the early problems of merchandizing, even to providing a counsellor ready to devote his entire time to establishing the new store on a sound foundation in the first months of its existence.

The auditing department of K.F. examines the accounts of

nearly all the local societies, a service which is available at the request of the local unit. Highly trained auditors, who have held various posts in the Union, visit the local societies at least twice a year, at the annual closing of accounts and at midyear stock-taking. Not only do they examine the accounts but, out of their long experience, they survey the whole field in which the society is operating, making any recommendations they consider necessary to the resident auditors, the store managers or the society's executive committee. Each month the societies send reports to K.F. so framed that the auditing department can determine at a glance the changes which may have occurred.

In 1923 there was formed what is in a sense a subsidiary of K.F., the Swedish Household Society, S.H.F. as it is familiarly known. Its function is to rescue coöperative stores that have not been successful under the direction of local societies. A salvage squad maintained by S.H.F. is equipped to step in and direct the business until it has improved to such a point that the local group is able to take it over again. S.H.F. grew out of the difficulties encountered by many coöperatives at the time of the post-war slump. In the opinion of coöperators it has proved its value many times over, restoring numerous failing societies to business health.

Although it is one of the largest business organizations in the country, K.F. is pervaded by a remarkable *esprit de corps* which even the outsider is quick to sense. The salaries are low in comparison with private business salaries. Albin Johansson, the director, receives, it is reported, less than 20,000 kronor a year, the equivalent roughly of somewhat more than $5,000 in this country. Other executive salaries are in proportion.

It is obvious that the men who direct this great enterprise are impelled by more than a monetary motive. They take a pride, which is not unlike a species of family pride, in the achievements of the organization. This is apparent as they show the visitor through the Tre Kronor mill that rises like a massive cliff above the blue water of Stockholm harbor, pointing out the latest machines and the newest and most efficient labor-saving devices. They are proud of their handsome new office building, completed less than a year ago and modern in every line and detail. It is an evidence of vitality that younger men are coming on to replace those who have built up the organization.

Foremost among the builders is Albin Johansson, president as well as managing director. Reserved and mild of manner, he is said by many to be the most astute merchant in the country. Conservatives pay him this tribute to explain away the success of coöperation—the fortunate accident that a business genius was at the head of the organization. Not out of modesty so much as out of his deep conviction of the value of coöperative methods, Johansson would be the first to reject this.

Johansson's rise in the coöperative movement was very rapid. Beginning as a shop clerk at the age of seventeen, with only a rudimentary education, he was advanced at the end of two years to the management of the store, founded by the workers in a sugar factory at Tanto, a part of Stockholm. Through intensive home study he had mastered cost accountancy and other fundamental business skills, and the rapid progress of the Tanto store was evidence of his managerial ability. This ability was soon recognized by K.F. When Johansson had been a store manager but two years, he was given a position in the parent organization. He soon established a close relationship with Martin Sundell, one of the most ardent pioneers of the coöperative movement. Together they worked tirelessly to advance the cause.

One of the weaknesses of the movement in 1916, as coöperators themselves were well aware, was the fact that the forces of coöperation in Stockholm were so divided. Johansson left K.F. at this time and undertook, as general manager of the largest Stockholm society, the difficult task of bringing the various factions together. It is due to his intensive efforts in 1916 and 1917 that the Stockholm Coöperative Society has grown to a position of such power, by far the largest distributor of foodstuffs in the capital. When it was possible to leave this job, Johansson returned to K.F., and with his return the coöperative movement in Sweden began a new and flourishing period of development. During 1917 and 1918 he undertook a thoroughgoing reorganization of K.F. At the end of that time he was advanced to the position of managing director of the Union.

Today he is one of the recognized leaders of the country, a member of the board of state railways—a position of the highest importance—on the board of the state opera, and in numerous other offices of trust and responsibility in public life. Johansson has his jealous detractors, of course. He is associated in many ways with the industrial leaders of the country and is consulted in all important issues. Recently in recognition of his position he was named to the crown prince's party visiting America for the tercentenary celebration. He lives modestly in a five-room house, so his critics cannot say that he enjoys a life of luxurious ease at the expense of the coöperative movement. Jealousy, incidentally, is one of the strongest traits of the Swedish character. It is referred to with a kind of pride, as "the royal Swedish jealousy." When a person of lofty rank receives a blow to his prestige or vanity there is a harsh saying: "Well, it will do no harm for him to be reminded that he is after all only mortal."

Johansson's passionate hatred of monopoly control—in fact of any barriers in restraint of free trade—has undoubtedly shaped the policy of the movement. He led the successive battles against the various cartels. This dislike of trusts and trade barriers extends to the international field, and the head of K.F. has been among those who have worked most intensively for an international wholesale coöperative society. His practical ability, extending to numerous improvements in production technique, is hardly less than his skill as a propagandist.

The splendid rapport which exists between the Union and the retail societies is said to be due in part at least to Johansson's never-failing awareness of the coöperative relationship. How well the two branches work together is shown by the way in which the shoe trade was reorganized in 1927.

After K.F. acquired a shoe factory, with a production of a thousand pairs a day, a special committee was appointed to revise this entire department of the business. The committee recommended that existing shops and all stock owned by local retail societies be transferred to K.F., the latter to create a chain of shoe stores which would sell at retail locally and at wholesale to neighboring societies outside the trade range of these specialized shops. Local societies would subscribe $3 a member in share capital to the undertaking, to be repaid as the new industry became self-supporting, and K.F. would pass along to the locals a rebate of 3 per cent on all retail shoe sales. With scarcely any argument, the annual congress approved this proposal, perhaps because a similar plan for the manufacture of spisbröd, the hard rye bread which is an essential of Swedish diet, had worked so well.

K.F. has always followed a conservative financial policy. While it has accumulated a considerable reserve, this has been kept as a margin of safety, a large part of it consisting of "production guarantee fund." Besides this, K.F. conducts a savings bank, for coöperators only, the local societies, except two or three of the larger ones, being merely branch offices to take deposits and pay out withdrawals. One way in which the movement encourages thrift is to make it easy for the dividend on purchases to accumulate in a savings account. Although K.F. has followed an extremely cautious policy with funds drawn from this source, it has nevertheless been a most useful credit reserve in the growth of the organization. From time to time, to finance a new venture, K.F. has offered its obligations direct to the public, and with a flattering response. It is one of the Union's proudest boasts that it has never had to resort to bank credit.

Coöperative insurance societies, most of them having come in recent years under the wing of K.F., have been very successful. The beginning was in 1908 with a society called Coöperation, organized for fire insurance alone. Burglary, fidelity, and motor insurance have been added. The total volume in these classifications is more than $250,000,000. Life insurance on a coöperative basis was undertaken first in 1914 by a special group, The People, which has since been taken over by K.F. More than 150,000 policy holders have nearly $50,000,000 of insurance in force.

The achievements of coöperation thus far have been in the face of bitter and unceasing opposition. Merchants, millers, manufacturers of every kind have banded together in groups

to defend their special interests with all the resources and all
the resourcefulness at their command. They have fought in the
courts, in the newspapers—wherever the issue could be raised.
At every opportunity they have employed shibboleths and catch
phrases to brand coöperation as sinister, insidious, a subtle device for undermining the home, the school, and religion.

When recently K.F. took over a large department store in
Stockholm and offered the employees all possible aid in form-
ing an independent union, in line with K.F.'s progressive labor
policy, the conservative newspapers in large headlines branded
this as a form of coercion. The employees were being coerced
into joining a radical union so that they would become a part
of the "battering ram" K.F. is fashioning to destroy the established order. Coöperation is the spearhead of socialism, of
revolution, the conservatives cry. But K.F. is not disturbed by
such outcries. Now when an organization of private merchants
buys a page in the newspapers to denounce the coöperatives,
the latter use the same medium to answer in kind. And so the
fight continues.

Coöperative leaders are proud that in the course of their long
struggle they have never appealed to the state for help. They
have been able to meet their competitors on an equal basis,
without seeking special privileges or favors. And yet in many
respects Swedish law has worked to the disadvantage of the
coöperatives and in the interest of privately owned stores.

This is particularly true with regard to taxation. Under Swedish law limited companies are taxed in proportion to profit and
share capital. But coöperative societies, *ekonomiska föreningar,*
are taxed on the same basis as individual taxpayers; that is in
proportion to their income on a gradual scale which rises
very sharply. It is for this reason that K.F. in taking over established businesses has allowed them to remain in the form
of independent limited companies. What the difference means
is shown by the fact that for the division of K.F. which is organized as a coöperative society in the legal sense, *ekonomisk
förening,* the taxes of various kinds amounted in 1932 to 608,-
000 kronor, whereas the tax would have been only 268,000
kronor if it had been at the rate paid by limited companies.

The Stockholm retail society organized its productive

branches as limited companies from the beginning in order to escape the higher tax. And this is not regarded as an attempt to circumvent the law, for the choice of legal forms, as between individual or collective enterprise, is a free one under the law. It remains true, however, that K.F. as well as the large retail societies pay proportionately much higher taxes because they are unable to organize their entire business in the limited form. Together with its affiliated companies, the factories and various productive enterprises retained as limited companies, K.F. in 1932 paid more than 1,200,000 kronor in taxes and local rates.

In this respect, too, Swedish coöperators like to point out the contrast with England. English coöperators, they say, have derived numerous advantages from special laws, particularly with regard to tax exemption. And it is true that the charge of tax favoritism is the cry most frequently raised against the British coöperatives by the conservative press.

If the coöperators are proud of their independence of the state, they are also proud of the fact, and they insist that it is a fact, of their independence of political parties. Their enemies have charged a close link with the Social-Democrats but the coöperators have always denied that such a connection exists. By virtue of common interests and, in certain instances, common leadership, the coöperatives are in fact closely allied with both the Social-Democrats and the trade unions. All three have, in a sense, the same objective. But the coöperators hold that coöperation is so general in its appeal as to be independent of class and political strife. And paradoxical as this may sound to those who think in traditional terms of class and party, the Swedes seem to have gone a long way toward proving it.

Why the large-scale capitalists in Sweden have not succeeded in striking down this upstart David is a question that inevitably occurs to the visitor from America. The coöperators' answer is that by a cautious, careful, pay-as-you-go method of finance they have been able to keep out of the capitalists' reach.

Swedish coöperators take a jealous pride in their financial independence. They resent even the suggestion that help may have come from outside sources, from capitalists or politicians In his attitude toward the broader economic issues Albin Johansson is essentially conservative. He speaks with admiration of "working capitalists" as opposed to "finance capitalists." The latter are responsible for the growth of monopolies, they have interfered with the proper functioning of the capitalist system. And there is reason to believe that the capitalist, or at any rate certain capitalists, look not only with tolerance but with approval upon the rise of the coöperative movement. They feel that it has had a salutary effect on the economy of the country.

It is not that Swedish coöperators are indifferent to the larger social and economic issues that their movement implies. It is, rather, that they are entirely preoccupied with immediate practical problems. At the annual congress for several years the delegate from one of the societies in the extreme north has been a Communist. Each time he takes the floor to denounce the surplus which accumulates as a reserve fund, demanding that it be reduced or done away with. The assembly pays him polite attention but the suggestion is not considered seriously—it is not practical.

A few of the local societies, and in particular that of Stockholm, have grown large enough and strong enough to wage war on the trusts on their own initiative. For several years the Stockholm society fought the price level fixed by Stockholm bakers. Having built and equipped the finest bakery in the country in 1923, K.F.S. was in a strategic position to attack bread prices. The latter were extortionate, a fact which was concealed by a multiplicity of kinds of bread, with varying weights and prices.

One of the coöperative society's first moves was to bring about an official investigation which proved beyond any doubt that bread prices of the private bakers, when comparable types were properly classified, were on the average 32 per cent higher than the coöp. prices. The average housekeeper saved nearly eight dollars a year, it was estimated, by buying her bread from K.F.S. At the same time that the results of this investigation were published, the society began a vigorous advertising campaign to boom two principal types of bread to be sold in loaves of one kilogram each. The result was that within a year private bakers had to modify their whole price policy, and adopt the standard size loaf introduced by K.F.S.

Considering the remarkable progress that consumers' coöp-

eration has made and the profound effect that it has had upon
the price level, upon purchasing power, upon the trend of capitalism, it seems strange to find that producers' coöperation has
been comparatively slow of growth. One reason may have been
the insistence of the Swedes upon "true coöperation," based
upon production for use upon a nonprofit basis. Producers' cooperatives do not come within this definition because, although
they are organized coöperatively, it is their function to sell on
the open market at a profit.

Agricultural coöperation has made considerable headway,
particularly in the field of dairying, following the example of
Denmark, where, as will be shown later, the coöperatives have
taken over almost the entire business of processing and marketing the products of the farm. In Sweden agricultural producers'
coöps. dominate the dairying industry, handling well over two
thirds of all the milk that is processed in factory dairies and
producing more than three fourths of all the butter, excluding
that which is made in small domestic dairies. As in Denmark,
the coöperative dairies have been of great value in developing
the export trade in butter. But Sweden has lacked the strong
central organization which has contributed so much to the
growth of the Danish dairying industry on a coöperative basis.

The misfortunes that beset an early venture, the National
Union of Swedish Farmers, may have had some retarding effect
upon rural coöperation. At one time, just before the World
War, this group boasted 83,000 members who had under cul-
tivation 14.7 per cent of the tillable land of the whole country.
But the prosperity that the war brought to agriculture was a
stimulus which led the Farmers' Union far afield, into banking,
and shipping on a scale that soon proved disastrous. The state
intervened to take over the bank and thereby salvage a part of
the farmers' losses.

K.F., which is strictly a consumers' organization, on the initiative of Albin Johansson, has done everything within its
power to aid the Farmers' Union. For example, when private
livestock dealers organized to fight the farmers' livestock coöp.,
K.F. stepped in, helped finance the latter and agreed to buy
all meats required by its member societies from this farmers'
coöperative. This provided a large and unfailing market which

went a long way to establish the farmers' livestock coöperative on a sound basis. And it meant that a considerable portion of the meat business was organized coöperatively all the way from the farmer to the consumer.

Again, when a cartel had succeeded in pegging the price of fertilizer at an exorbitant level, K.F., with its superior resources, stepped in and bought a superphosphate factory in the neighborhood of Stockholm with a capacity of 500,000 sacks a year. During the first year, 1928 to 1929, this was operated jointly by K.F. and the Farmers' Union and in that year the price was forced down so successfully that the farmers of the country realized total savings of from one and a half to two million kronor. In November of 1931, K.F. leased the superphosphate factory to the Farmers' Union.

These and other steps that K.F. has taken on behalf of the farmer have served indirectly to advance consumers' coöperation among the rural population. Of the 550,675 members affiliated with K.F., 19 per cent are farmers. This represents a much higher proportion of the farm population than was affiliated with K.F. in the early years.

The coöperative movement in Sweden has in general been free of proselytism. It has not been a "movement" at all in the now slightly absurd connotation of that word. Rather, as will appear, when coöperation has been the logical solution in housing, in the distribution of power, in agriculture, then that form has been adopted and its growth has been healthy and rapid.

Thus the coöperative Milk Central, supplying nearly three fourths of all the dairy products consumed in Stockholm, came out of an investigation by the Stockholm City Council into high milk prices. A special committee was named to plan a municipal milk supply in coöperation with the producers, eliminating the "costly and unnecessary middleman." The four principal companies were merged and formed into a producers' coöperative society.

The turnover of the Milk Central was more than doubled in ten years' time. And the coöperative, dominating the field, set standards for purity and excellence which other dairies were compelled to follow. The Milk Central has dominated prices, too, and with a resulting gain to consumers that has not been small. The low price is probably the most important factor in Stockholm's high milk consumption.

There are about 8,000 members of this largest producers' coöperative and they own the largest and most modern dairy in the country. The Milk Central maintains its own inspection service which follows the product from the cow to the consumer. Of the milk received, 43 per cent goes into direct consumption, 28 per cent into the manufacture of cheese and 29 per cent to butter. Butter sales in recent years have amounted to more than 4,000 tons annually, most of which has gone into domestic consumption, and the production of cheese has been close to 6,000 tons a year. The direction of this extensive business is in the hands of a management committee, from which an executive board of six is named to act with the paid director. There are also local representatives with voting rights in all the districts around Stockholm from which the milk supply is drawn.

There is evidence that the growing interest of the farm population in both producer and consumer coöperation will continue. K.F. is moving in new directions to make sure that it will continue. A plan whereby K.F. provided grain elevators in which farmers stored their wheat, so that at the harvest it was not of necessity dumped onto the market to the destruction of the price level, functioned for some years. Now the government undertakes to stabilize the domestic price for grain along the line of the McNary-Haugen plan.

That this cycle may some day be completed, with the elimination of all profit from production, would seem to be prophesied by the rapid development of the coöperative movement. But this is hardly more than a premise with which Swedish coöperators are not just now concerned. The following statement by Axel Gjöres is perhaps as near as Swedish coöperators ever come to a discussion of the future in generalized terms:

The strictly limited view that Swedish coöperation holds of its functions, clearly visible in all its methods and efforts, may very probably seem narrow to those whose coöperative philosophy has taken other directions and forms, but in point of fact it gives to the movement the widest scope conceivable. A coöperative movement, which in its every phase holds fast by the consumer interest and resolutely refuses every commitment that does not directly and irresistibly derive therefrom is, in the real meaning of the term, open to all, and is in a position to enlist in its ranks the greater part of the nation.

III

BREAKING AN INTERNATIONAL MONOPOLY

COOPERATIVE distribution and production having attained a strong, well-integrated growth within national boundaries, it was natural to seek to carry the idea a logical step forward. If it worked nationally, why would it not work internationally? Coöperators in Europe had been thinking in this direction for many years; this was a large hope cherished long before the outbreak of the World War. It was out of the war, with the enormous difficulties it put in the way of European trade, that the first international coöperative developed.

After 1914 the wholesale societies of Sweden, Norway, and Denmark had been hard put to it to import certain essential supplies. The North Sea was mined and blockaded. The great warring powers, engrossed in supplying their own combatants with essential foods, were indifferent to the trading problems of small nations on the edge of the European inferno. It was only through tact, patience, and the most painstaking effort that the Scandinavian countries were able to import any quantity at all of coffee, rice, sugar, and other products necessarily obtained from abroad.

Out of this common experience there was created Nordisk Andölsforbund, the Scandinavian Coöperative Wholesale. It was on the initiative of Albin Johansson that the first meeting of representatives of the coöperative movement from the Scandinavian countries and Finland was held in 1918. Delegates at that first meeting brought up a wide variety of proposals. Some wanted a coöperatively owned orange grove in California. Others were for starting a coöperative shipping line. In the end a modest and practical plan prevailed.

It was decided to form a Scandinavian coöperative agency, with headquarters in Copenhagen and with one of the leaders of the Danish Wholesale Society as manager. The choice of

Copenhagen seemed obvious, partly because coöperation was at that time more highly developed in Denmark than in the rest of Scandinavia, but above all because it is the most strategically located of the Scandinavian capitals. The primary purpose of Nordisk Andölsforbund, customarily shortened to N.A.F., was to eliminate the middleman—the commission man —intervening between buyer and seller, and by eliminating his profit to cut down the cost of goods necessarily imported into Scandinavian countries. The members of N.A.F. are: Kooperativa Förbundet, Sweden; the Danish Coöperative Wholesale Society; the two Finnish wholesales, S.O.K. and O.T.K.; and the Norwegian Coöperative Wholesale Society.

At the start N.A.F. was fortunate in its manager, Frederik Nielsen, who had been for many years head of the colonial department of the Danish Wholesale Society. He brought to his new job a thoroughgoing knowledge of foreign trade. And for some time he retained his former post, thus assuring the closest collaboration between N.A.F. and its then largest customer, the Danish society.

N.A.F. makes purchases for the respective accounts of its five members. In relation to the foreign producers N.A.F. is thus actually the buyer and not merely the agent. But since N.A.F. buys only on the order of its members and so never receives goods or stores them, its position is like that of any agent or middleman in private business. In most instances the foreign producers are paid directly by the wholesale society purchasing the produce, N.A.F. receiving from the seller the commission of an agent. Establishing offices in London, it was not long before the new international society had developed a considerable volume of business.

At the end of the sixth year the annual turnover was more than $6,000,000. From the beginning nearly half of N.A.F.'s sales have been in coffee, imported from Brazil, Central America, and the Far East. The society is in direct touch with large producing and exporting firms in the coffee countries as well as with the European branches of other firms and is therefore in a position to bargain for the most favorable price.

The other principal groups of commodities in which N.A.F. deals are grain and flour, including rice, sago, and tapioca as well as wheat flour, fruits, margarine oils, bacon and lard, and syrup. Direct contact is maintained with large American flour mills, for the most part on behalf of the Danish Wholesale Society. California, Spain, and Bosnia are the important sources from which N.A.F. imports various fruits, both dried and fresh. Vegetable oils for the manufacture of margarine, largely for the Swedish society, are obtained from European refineries. Coöperators in Scandinavia have long looked forward to a favorable opportunity when they might establish their own coöperative refineries and thus go direct to the producers of raw materials.

N.A.F.'s total sales during 1934 were 32,000,000 kronor. This had increased in 1935 to 45,231,452 and by 1936 it was 50,807,317. The chief commodities bought and sold were: cotton seed and other vegetable products yielding oil, 98,533 tons; sugar, 20,985 tons; coffee, 15,682 tons; grain and cattle fodder, 10,106 tons; salt, 7,748 tons; dried fruit, 5,151 tons. The total sales in 1936 were distributed between different members as follows: Sweden, 31,517,812 kronor; Denmark, 8,191,412; Finland, S.O.K., 4,616,733, O.T.K., 4,990,277; and Norway, 1,491,080. The surplus is distributed in accord with coöperative principles and put aside as a reserve fund on the respective accounts of the member wholesales.

In the first five years of its existence N.A.F. saved Scandinavian coöperative consumers about $250,000. It was not a large amount, this "profit" achieved through the collaboration of the four countries, but the coöperative leaders were more than satisfied with the promise of N.A.F. For this was in a sense an incidental saving. And it was the first international coöperative in the true sense, the national wholesale societies of four countries coöperating in world trade. The partners were, to be sure, people of rather similar racial background, their respective countries forming a single closely integrated area. But nevertheless the fact remains that they first succeeded in crossing national boundaries to coöperate in the distribution of goods for use and not for profit.

Certain coöperative leaders, observing the economies effected by cutting out the middleman, proposed that N.A.F. might do well to purchase and develop its own coffee plantations. The

English and Scottish wholesale societies, they pointed out, owned large tea plantations in India and Ceylon. But on serious consideration it was decided that the potential savings from such a project would not justify the necessary investment and consequent risk. Half the supply of coffee for Scandinavian coöperators came from Brazil, and the government of Brazil had to a certain degree made coffee production a state monopoly; production at any rate was on such a highly organized basis that a single plantation could hardly hope to achieve important economies. Plain common sense dictated against a venture in Brazil.

Many European coöperatives were engaged in the field of international trade. As early as 1908, the English Coöperative Wholesale Society had established an export department to try to interest coöperative organizations in other countries in buying goods produced in coöperative factories in England. Not until after the war did this department really begin to function on a large scale. Then in other countries, too, the idea was taken up and an international committee was formed to study the problems involved in an international coöperative exchange. Representatives of the leading wholesale societies of Europe, meeting in April of 1920, adopted a resolution urging that every society set up an export department to find suitable markets for the "surplus production" that might arise in factories operated by the various societies.

To Swedish coöperators this seemed at the time a dangerous departure from true coöperative principles. They recognized that because of the economic crisis which followed the war coöperative industries could operate at only a fraction of their capacity. But regardless, the idea of a "surplus production" offered for sale at an outright profit to coöperators and to noncoöperators on the open market seemed at variance with all that coöperation stood for. Anders Hedberg, perhaps the leading theorist of Sweden's Coöperative Union, challenged this plan for the sale of surplus products with especial vigor.

It would inevitably lead, he argued, to the same kind of nationalistic competition that had developed under private production. It might even intensify this competition since under coöperative production a far larger number of individuals would have a stake in the profits to be realized from foreign trade. And yet, an ardent coöperator, Hedberg was keenly aware of what true coöperation might achieve in the international sphere.

As an example of the dangers implied in surplus production within a coöperative system, Hedberg pointed to what had happened in Finland where a very large proportion of all business is on a coöperative basis. Finnish coöperators were divided into two distinct camps, S.O.K., the elder society, and O.T.K. S.O.K. built a match factory. After it had been running for some time it was realized that because of the size of the factory and the nature of the business, production would have to be considerably increased to avoid serious losses. S.O.K.'s own membership could not absorb any more matches and O.T.K. was not a customer so there was nothing to do but look for markets abroad. Immediately, of course, the society came up against a powerful international trust, controlling at that time nearly 75 per cent of the world match industry.

The Finnish society was hardly equipped to combat such a powerful, hydra-headed rival. In typical fashion the trust began to cut prices to ruinous levels within limited areas both in Finland and abroad, seeking by that method to lure away the society's largest customers. But the members of S.O.K. remained loyal, spurning the trust's cheap matches. And so did the wholesale societies, in England and on the continent, that had begun to buy these coöperative matches from Finland. The directors of the Finnish society were extremely grateful for this loyalty which enabled them to operate their factory at a fair margin of profit.

But seeing the success of their rival in the match business, the members of O.T.K. decided that they, too, would build a match factory. They planned it from the start with a capacity considerably in excess of the needs of the members and were prepared upon its completion to compete in the foreign field. What followed appears to have been almost inevitable. The two societies entered into a disastrous competition for the coöperative trade of Europe. It was no longer a question of loyalty as between the trust and a coöperative. European wholesales bought their matches from the society that offered the lowest price. This competition seriously weakened the financial position of both S.O.K. and O.T.K.

The lesson in this, as Hedberg read it, was obvious. "Buying and selling between national central organizations cannot be regarded as a coöperative operation," Hedberg insisted, "and such a system does not form any true basis on which to build international coöperation." But sooner or later, he foresaw, the coöperatives would come up against other international trusts and unless their control over prices could be broken by true coöperative methods, the movement would have reached the limit of its usefulness.

Hedberg gave up a promising career in the army to become a coöperator. A brilliant thinker, he has at the same time a firm grasp on economic realities. His mind was occupied with the problem of finding some base for establishing, on however modest a scale, a system of production for use, between nations. Aware of the manifold obstacles—customs barriers, national jealousies, the chaotic state of post-war Europe—he still believed that it should be possible to make a beginning. And the increasing number of essential products that were coming under monopoly control of the great international trusts made it imperative, in his opinion, to find a way to begin.

"The efforts of government to cope with the harmful influences of the trust system have largely proved in vain," he wrote in 1925. "Laws have been passed and prohibitions imposed without any other result being achieved than that the trusts have proceeded along secret lines. Antitrust legislation has, as is realized nowadays in ever-widening circles, certain directly injurious effects from the very fact that it stimulates monopolistic combines to evade even that control which public opinion nevertheless can to some extent exercise if these combines show themselves in the open."

Meanwhile the Scandinavian Wholesale Society had continued to grow rapidly. But this was merely a wholesale agency, and while it was an important achievement, an important "first," Hedberg looked forward to a system of production on the same, or even a broader, international basis.

To one of the most conspicuous trusts, with price control that was worldwide and iron clad, Hedberg began to give serious thought. This was the cartel that dictated throughout Europe and America the manufacture of electric light bulbs. In thoroughgoing fashion Hedberg traced this trust down to its origins in 1902 when representatives of the leading European countries, speaking for 90 per cent of the total electric bulb production at that time, met in Berlin to establish production quotas. After certain differences had been settled, the delegates signed a contract that specified minutely all the details of production, regulating the distribution of profits, providing for the reallotment of production quotas in the event of strikes or other emergencies and fixing heavy penalties for violation of the terms of this extraordinary contract. As an example of how production was limited, the United Electricity Company of Vienna was shown to have produced 4,000,000 lamps in 1902 and its annual quota was therefore fixed at 3,100,000.

But this was trivial in comparison with the international trust that was formed after the war. The General Electric Company—American capital—working through the International General Electric Company founded a world-wide combine. First there were a series of companies that General Electric held outright as subsidiaries. Then there were other companies in which the great G.E. had acquired an important, if not a dominant, interest. And finally there were those companies to which the American firm had extended financial aid in time of stress. In one of his earliest reports to the Coöperative Union, Hedberg wrote:

By the beginning of the century control of the lamp industry in the United States was definitely concentrated in the General Electric Company. Manufacture proceeded partly in G.E.C. factories, partly in the factories of other firms dependent upon and operating under license from the G.E.C. Gradually a very extensive system of price agreements was thus built up, in strict secrecy; out of deference to the anti-trust laws a semblance of free competition was maintained. Finally, however, the law was invoked against the G.E.C., but not until 1911.

As a result, all manufacturers' agreements for the regulation of markets and the control of prices were declared illegal and undertakings were demanded that they should not be repeated. Sale contracts fixing retail prices were also declared contrary to law. Thus drastic changes were made necessary in the lamp industry. Companies working under G.E.C. license were dissolved and their manufacture then taken over by the G.E.C.! Sales policy was altered so that the manufacturer sold direct to the ultimate consumer, wholesalers and retailers functioning as agents of the manufacturers, handling only on consignment.

Legal proceedings had thus served merely in the long run to consolidate the electric lamp industry still more thoroughly. Price agreements between factories violated the law, but not so the purchase of one factory by another. And though the manufacturer might not dictate the price an independent retailer should charge, he overcame that difficulty by making the retailer his agent, selling for him. The whole story is an excellent example of the difficulty of combating the trust effectively by means of legislation.

Hedberg's researches, which took him to many European countries, brought out clearly how the trust had extended its power, levying tribute from consumers around the world. Interlocking patent agreements made it virtually impossible for an outsider to encroach upon this enormously profitable domain. But Hedberg became more and more convinced that the lamp trust could not be ignored; that, hopeless as it might seem on the face of it, coöperation, and, if necessary, Swedish coöperation, would have to confront the reality of price dictation in this field. The price variations from country to country were utterly irrational, based, it seemed to Hedberg, upon the simple precept of charging whatever the traffic would bear. The price in 1928 for a 25-watt lamp was 37 cents in Sweden, 30 cents in Holland and Germany, 27 cents in Denmark, as low as 18 cents in Hungary, and 52 cents in England.

For many months Swedish coöperators, inspired by Hedberg, considered what they might do. Careful calculation showed that the capital outlay required for a lamp factory was not beyond the reach of Swedish coöperation, amounting to less than the monthly net surplus of the Coöperative Union. But there was one vital question to be answered and that was whether the capital which would be tied up in a coöperative lamp factory might not be used to the greater advantage of consumers in some other way.

It was true that electric lamps played a relatively small part in the economy of the average household and therefore it seemed that the potential saving would be small. And yet a reduction of 12 cents in the price of a lamp would mean $1,500,000 saved to the consumers of the 12,000,000 lamps sold each year in Sweden. This looked worth while. And just at this time, in 1928, came an opportunity that was too rare to miss.

The Osram Lamp Company, a German corporation dominated by General Electric, had secured complete control of the Stockholm electric lamp factory, which was already a member of the international Phoebus Company, incorporated in Switzerland for the purpose of policing the lamp monopoly. Osram decided that the technical director of the Stockholm factory, H. Schlott, would be more useful in Berlin and consequently ordered him to return. But Mr. Schlott, indoctrinated with a stubborn Swedish pride, and having for a long time been more or less his own master, declined to be ordered about in this peremptory fashion. The alternative was to leave the company.

The Coöperative Union heard of his resignation and made a sudden decision. Hedberg and Johansson were well aware that technicians of sufficient skill to direct the construction and subsequent operation of a lamp factory, one of the most complex forms of mass production, are rare indeed. Most of them are tied by long-term contracts to the trust. They hired Mr. Schlott and commissioned him to build a coöperative factory. No time was lost and soon the walls of the new plant began to rise. Machinery was bought or specially designed, and the directors of K.F. began to lie awake nights wondering whether or not they had been rash.

The cartel heard of this absurd presumption in the north of Europe and began to inquire what it might mean. First, apparently on the theory that any opposition was undesirable, they held out tempting offers to Schlott to abandon the foolish venture. Then Phoebus developed a deep solicitude for these mistaken coöperators and Hedberg was persuaded to come to Geneva for a conference with one of the managing directors. It was David in the very tent of Goliath and a calm and collected David judging from Hedberg's report of the conversation to his fellow coöperators.

"You don't expect me to reveal the secrets of our organization, do you?" said Director Oppenheim after the first preliminary skirmish.

"We are hardly as simple as that," said Hedberg, "but we, of the Swedish Coöperative Wholesale Society, have at least one interest in common with you, and that is that only the truth should be told about Phoebus. So I would like to know if there are not mistakes, quite unintentional possibly, in the published reports of Dr. Meinhardt's addresses. [The first president of Phoebus, a representative of Osram, who made many outspoken statements about the purposes of the cartel.] Because his utterances are our principal source of information about Phoebus. Does he express the cartel point of view?"

"Certainly. We subscribe to every word he has said, and the reports, so far as I know, are perfectly correct [concerning the intention of the cartel to push prices higher]. But are you really going to build a factory? If it's only the prices that are too high, we can meet you on that. You won't find us difficult. But we must keep our market in Sweden; we can't agree to any new factory there. Of late years we have learned a lot from America; there they either come to an agreement of some sort with outside factories, that is, they buy them in one way or another, or they wipe them off the map. Up till now the same party has always won; the American G.E.C. is a powerful body, as you know. But we, in Europe, are not so far behind, and so I tell you quite candidly that no new factory will poach on our preserves in the Swedish market if we can prevent it. There might be very, very low prices in Sweden! Have a cigarette?"

"Thanks, I will; and thanks for the considerate manner in which you threaten. But, bear in mind, there is a vast difference between the *consumers'* coöperative factory and your other competitors. We don't mind your dumping lamps into Sweden. That is in the interests of the consumers, our clients. If you want to sell the Swedish people lamps below cost, or even give them away free, we shall applaud and thank you and congratulate ourselves on having built a factory that elicited such generosity."

"Quite noble! But I suppose you would like to get interest on your capital?"

"Surely! But our capital belongs to the consumers. The

money that Swedish consumers invest in an electric lamp factory is amply remunerated by a reduction in lamp prices; cannot, indeed, be better remunerated."

"We shall see about that; time will tell. Now, can't we write our representative in Sweden instructing him to get in touch with your people and try to come to terms? We can make it worth your while not to start that factory."

"No use discussing that! We have tried for years, and in vain, to persuade manufacturers to reduce their prices, and you have ignored the price question until now, when the Swedish Wholesale Society has decided to build its own factory and until you learn that we have secured a capable manager. Our decision will assuredly stand."

"But why? Decisions are easily enough rescinded. And don't you think there are enough lamp factories already in Sweden?"

"Can't say I do. But perhaps you mean that you will sell us one of the cartel factories—the one in Stockholm or that at Nyköping . . .?"

"Oh, no, no! What I mean is that lamp prices may fall *very* low in Sweden—see? And that won't please any of us."

"Why not? Our principal desire and object is to get prices down. You and I represent two totally different interests, so that we have great difficulty understanding each other; you want prices up, we want them down; you want to benefit stockholders, we want to benefit consumers."

"You're not really serious, are you?"

"Wait and see!"

From the first it had been planned that coöperators of all northern countries should present a united front against the Phoebus cartel. At preliminary conferences representatives of the wholesale societies of Denmark, Finland, Norway, and Sweden had agreed to combine forces. And as construction of the factory went forward, nominally at the expense of the Swedish society, these preliminary conferences were continued. Shortly after the plant was completed, delegates from the four countries met again to form the North European Luma Coöperative Society. On May 28, 1931, this international coöperative took over the plant and production was begun.

It is a true coöperative in every sense, with ownership in the five coöperative wholesale societies. Ultimate authority is vested in a general meeting in which each of the societies has the same voting right. In the interval between annual meetings the management is intrusted to a supervisory council and a board of managers. The council, made up of representatives of the five societies, outlines the duties and supervises the work of the two managers in whom is vested sole legal responsibility.

The effect on the price of electric bulbs in Scándinavia was startling. Even while the Luma plant was in course of construction, the trust lowered the Swedish price from 37 cents to 27 cents. Soon after the coöperative lamp came on the market the trust had to meet the Luma price of 22 cents. This price allowed for a comfortable margin of surplus—a safe margin, the council felt. The trust threatened patent suits. But before the coöperators began to build their plant, they made sure that essential patents had expired and they felt they were running only a minor legal risk.

So remarkable was Luma's success that English coöperators began to discuss the possibility of a similar venture. And promptly the price of light bulbs in England dropped about ten cents. In the first year of its operation the Luma plant turned out nearly 3,000,000 lamps. The "profit" on this production, with the exception of sufficient bookkeeping reserves, was paid out in dividends to the purchasers of the three million lamps through the five member wholesales. There were suggestions from several sources that the capacity of Luma should be increased and that it should then export coöperative lamps to European wholesale societies. But these suggestions were never seriously considered, for, although such an export trade might have been entirely feasible, this would have put the international society in competition on a profit-making basis with private industry.

By various means the coöperative leaders in Scandinavia sought to make consumers understand the true significance of Luma's success and the advantages to be realized from coöperation. For example, one large colored poster advertising Luma bulbs included a graph showing how the price charged by the trust dropped even before the Luma plant went into operation.

Another poster carried the price paid in England and the price paid in Sweden for the same bulb, the significant difference of nearly twenty-five cents being the gain from coöperation. Still another poster pointed out that the Luma bulbs were manufactured to test for 1,500 hours and the trust's lamps for 1,000 hours.

Hedberg wrote in a pamphlet:

But even greater importance attaches to Luma as a practical example of the coöperative movement's power, disregarding national boundaries, to set up industrial undertakings to be owned in common by several national coöperative wholesale societies. Such international coöperation is urgently needed in these days in several fields; the private manufacturers are steadily being welded more and more into vast international combines; too often with monopolist aspirations. Against these the coöperative movement is powerless if it cannot overcome its nationalism.

Just as the local stores need their common national wholesale society to provide supplies and to manufacture more efficiently and economically, so do the national wholesales in their turn need common international enterprises for defending the consumers against the ever-increasing powers of international trusts and cartels. The fight against monopoly and monopolist proclivities cannot be waged to any purpose with tumult and with shouting, nor with sonorous phrases and big words. The unwearying, inconspicuous toil on details and the stubborn, resolute cohesion that have hitherto brought victory and progress to the coöperative standard continue the soundest tactics in this larger field.

Production during the second year, 1934, showed a very satisfactory increase. Total purchase of Luma lamps rose from 1,340,000 kronor in 1933 to 1,810,000 in 1934. In the second year Luma turned out approximately 3,500,000 lamps, an increase of about 30 per cent. Besides ordinary bulbs for household use Luma now manufactures motor car lamps and a half dozen other special types. During the second year there were no price increases. On the basis of price reduction brought about through the inception of Luma, the coöperatives can claim, and with good reason, a saving to the consuming public of five million kronor a year, realized on the ten million lamps sold annually.

At the present rate of production Luma is able to satisfy about one third of the total demand for electric lamps in Sweden. Actually in 1934 the coöperative plant supplied about 22 per cent of Swedish demand. The balance of Sweden's share of the production was exported to the Argentine, Brazil, Iceland, Egypt, and Bulgaria in exchange for goods imported by Kooperativa Förbundet. And a certain proportion of Luma lamps in Sweden, Norway, Denmark, and Finland are sold to noncoöperative customers.

This last is a significant development. During the past few years, as coöperators have ventured into more and more complex fields of production, there has risen the issue of whether it is possible to deviate from the line of true coöperation, into the sphere of profit making, and yet maintain the fundamental basis on which the movement was founded. It has proved difficult, or impossible, to plan production, in those fields in which large scale operation is essential, in such a way that the entire output will be absorbed at the start by coöperative buyers. And yet it was in those very fields that monopoly challenged the progress of the coöperatives. The leaders of the movement felt compelled to accept that challenge although they were well aware that they were venturing upon a dubious and even dangerous course.

The first venture into mass production requiring sales far beyond the limits of the coöperative movement came about with the purchase by K.F. in 1932 of a vegetable oil factory in the south of Sweden. The reason for this new venture and the circumstances surrounding it illustrate the present course of the coöperative movement in Sweden and show what may be its chief function in the national economy.

The Karlshamn plant was constructed by private business in 1928 outside the powerful European oil and margarine combine, "Unilever." And immediately after it began production, of course, it encountered a kind of competition that no independent company with limited resources can meet. "Unilever" simply cut prices below cost in those trade areas where the new company had begun to make inroads. The Swedish firm was inevitably forced out of business.

K.F., at Johansson's initiative, came to the rescue. Coöperators could not ignore the existence of a combine that was in a position to dominate the price of an essential food supply, Johansson and the other leaders argued. This was the familiar argument brought forward in the past on behalf of those earlier and smaller experiments in production. But now it was proposed that K.F. join forces with other elements within the country, certain private interests, that were also desirous of breaking the hold of the trust. And it was on the basis of a more or less clear understanding with the other interests that K.F. entered the deal for the Karlshamn plant.

What the coöperative directors said, in effect, was this. Here is an international trust that is harmful to our national economy. Because of the very nature of production in this field, it cannot be undertaken on a wholly coöperative basis; production to be profitable must be on so large a scale that coöperative consumers alone could never buy the output. Nevertheless we cannot overlook the fact that this combine is able to create an artificial price level for a commodity essential to almost every citizen in the land. Therefore the time has come to unite with other forces that are seeking to break this combine.

That was the theory. Beginning with an understanding with private business in Sweden, K.F. proceeded on a vigorous campaign to line up every group that might have an interest in seeing the power of the trust broken, both at home among coöperators and noncoöperators and abroad among coöperative organizations. The Karlshamn plant was large and modern in every respect, and K.F. began with a production schedule on a scale that assumed the greater proportion of the output would be sold to private business. Thus although it would supply all the oil required by K.F.'s own margarine factory this would be but a small fraction of the output.

In the first two years of operation the Karlshamn plant has been so successful that its activities have been expanded. It has returned a profit, most of which has gone into K.F.'s reserve fund as capital for other future ventures. While there is no record of exactly how much has gone into channels of private trade, the following table, showing the distribution of production in 1933, expressed in metric tons, makes clear what a small proportion of the total output has been absorbed by Swedish coöperators:

CATTLE FODDER

Export to coöperative organizations and private customers abroad	Sales to private customers in Sweden	Kooperativa Förbundet and some Swedish consumers' coöperative societies	National Union of Farmers' Coöperative Purchasing Societies	TOTAL
40,263	12,617	2,751	5,366	60,997

OIL

4,475	8,238	7,995	None	20,708

How much of the 40,263 tons in the first column went to private purchasers and how much to coöperators is not specified but considerably more than half of what was absorbed in Sweden went into private trade. In 1934 the total output of the Karlshamn plant was increased to 112,000 tons, of which 53,000 were exported to twenty-two different countries. This has been accomplished, coöperative leaders point out, without tariff or any kind of state subsidy, either direct or indirect.

Under similar circumstances K.F. undertook the manufacture of cash registers, marking a departure, and a radical departure it is, from the production of consumer goods to the production of capital goods. Here, too, a powerful international combine, dominated by the National Cash Register Company in the United States and the Krupp interests in Germany, was responsible, coöperative leaders believed, for fixing the price level. The price of cash registers in Sweden was extremely high and therefore, as early as 1928, K.F. put technicians to work to determine the feasibility of perfecting and manufacturing a cash register for the Swedish market.

In 1932 the first cash register was turned out by this new coöperative industry. Two years later production was at the rate of forty-two a week. The different parts of the machine are made by engineering firms in various parts of Sweden and the parts are then sent to Stockholm to be assembled in the coöperative factory. K.F. is at present able to sell its cash register for about half the price charged by the National Cash Register–Krupp combine. Here again coöperative enterprise was not large enough to absorb the entire output and even before beginning manufacture, private business firms. were appealed to. Production was held at a fairly stable level, about forty units a week, until the middle of 1937 when a larger factory was acquired and plans completed for expansion.

The K.F. cash register has been sold in Finland, Norway, Denmark, Czechoslovakia, France, and Great Britain, chiefly to coöperative organizations. Virtually no sales overhead is involved. K.F. has a close relationship with coöperative units in all European countries; their objective is the same; it is merely necessary to state the price and the workmanship of the machine. Numerous inquiries have come from other countries and even American coöperators traveling in Sweden have inquired about the possibility of importing coöperative cash registers.

K.F. is just now undergoing a phase of extraordinary expansion. Production of tires, and particularly bicycle tires, at the Gislaved factory has been increased during the last few years, with a total output from 1932 to 1934 inclusive of 140,000 automobile tires. In 1933 K.F. acquired a second rubber factory, at Viskafors, employing 350 workers against the 1,100 at Gislaved. But in the first year under K.F. the number of employees at Viskafors was increased to 491. The latter plant specializes in rubber soles, rubber heels, and other units for K.F.'s shoe factories. As with the oil plant and the cash register factory, production is on a scale that calls for some exports, either to coöperators or noncoöperators, and for domestic sales outside the limits of the coöperative movement.

In the boldest stroke thus far, K.F. in June of 1935 acquired one of the two largest department stores in Stockholm, Paul U. Bergström's, known to the Stockholm shopper as PUB. This is second in size only to the great Nordiska Kompaniet and is just as modern and efficient as N.K. Clearly under coöperative ownership and management PUB will draw a considerable proportion of its customers from outside the limits of the coöperative societies. Consumers in Stockholm are looking forward to the sharpest competition between the two institutions. And coöperative leaders are confident that this latest move will draw thousands of new members into the coöperative ranks. They will become members in order to receive the patronage dividend to which only members are entitled as well as the benefit of lower prices that will draw them in the first instance to PUB. At the outset K.F. will have the advantage of a loyal staff of employees built up through the intelligent labor policy of the private owners of the store.

And in still another direction K.F. proposes to expand. At the 1934 congress of coöperative delegates the management council and board of directors were authorized "to determine by what methods the movement can most suitably support Swedish handcrafts." K.F. has taken the first step in proposing a new kind of export group in which the General Export Association of Sweden and the Swedish Handcrafts Organization would coöperate. At the present stage of development it is not clear just how closely this will be related to the coöperative movement. In part it is undoubtedly an expression of Albin Johansson's concern over the fate of the craftsman and the well-being of the entire economy in which the craftsman must find a place.

K.F. has offered to contribute 500,000 kronor to this new organization and has suggested a general outline to be followed, based upon trade relations that already exist with private and coöperative groups throughout the world. K.F. has proposed the publication at regular intervals of a trade journal, in the nature of a catalogue of the craftsman's wares, to be printed in English, French, German, and Spanish. This publication would contain advertisements to be inserted by potential exporters who would pay for these advertisements out of the proceeds of the first sales. In addition to free publication of advertisements in this catalogue, members of the organization would receive all available information about market conditions, price levels, and so forth.

Private industrial and handcraft groups may become members of the organization by contributing capital of not less than one hundred kronor. K.F. has agreed to furnish the necessary additional capital to make up a minimum sum required to start the organization; this would be within the limits of K.F.'s original offer of 500,000 kronor. The General Export Association has given the idea favorable recommendation in a report that calls attention to the success of an earlier export scheme in which K.F. collaborated with private business to exchange produce with Persia. Hundreds of applications and promises of capital were received as soon as the latest plan was made public.

Coöperative leaders have shown an increasing tendency to collaborate with private business when they feel that such collaboration is in the interest of the consuming public. As one justification for the organization to improve the position of the craftsman, K.F. can point to the fact that there are 50,000 craftsmen who belong to coöperative societies.

Concern over the wisdom of these newest moves found expression at the 1934 Congress of K.F. A committee was appointed to study the problem. While the report of this committee offers no solution, it made plain difficulties of organization that must be met. The committee reached the conclusion that the coöperative movement had achieved so much power and so extensive a capital that it must undertake further ventures in the interest of the national economy. At the same time the report emphasized that it was essential that these new ventures conform with the financial principle on which the coöperative movement is based; that is, that all activities must be financed out of the organization's own capital and not out of borrowed funds; and furthermore that these outside activities shall never become so extensive as to overshadow the primary function of coöperation, which is to provide its members with the goods they need. The committee submitted the following resolution which was unanimously adopted by the Congress.

The Thirty-fifth Congress of the Coöperative Union instructs the management of the Union and recommends that the affiliated societies:

Devote their united and persistent efforts to combating monopolistic associations which abuse their power of controlling prices;

Strengthen and develop fruitful coöperation between farmers and the distributive coöperative movement;

Study the means by which the coöperative movement can best assist Swedish handcrafts;

Coöperate with the other elements that make up the Swedish economy in those spheres in which the coöperative movement has important interests to protect and in which united efforts are necessary to render services to the whole of the economic system.

The Congress also instructs the Central Board and Executive Committee of the Union to examine more closely the question of the form of organization for the collaboration of the coöperative movement with the other elements in the national economy in order that the coöperative principle concerning the purchasers' right to membership and to a share in the profits of the undertaking from which they buy their goods may be safeguarded.

The last paragraph in particular shows what the leaders of the movement consider its function to be. But this is shown even more clearly in the courses of study offered by the organization known as the Coöperative Groups. There is a general analogy between the rôle of the Groups in the coöperative movement and the rôle of the Communist party in Russia. They are centers where the ideology of coöperation, of production for use, is focused and through which new ideas and trends are passed along to the mass of coöperators. The Groups are in a sense cells for the discussion and clarification of coöperative principles and policies, and in part, too, for the dissemination of propaganda. At the start too much was left to spontaneous enthusiasm and good will in the formation of the Groups. Axel Gjöres had brought the idea for the Groups from England after extended study of coöperative methods there, and it was assumed that it would be sufficient merely to issue a call for the formation of such centers. While some Groups were formed it was soon discovered that a more definite plan was necessary and above all a link with the central organization was essential. With this in mind the Groups were reorganized, somewhat along the lines of the highly successful correspondence school which K.F. started thirteen years ago and which had enrolled in 1935 38,000 students in more than a hundred courses.

The new Groups were built around a definite series of courses, in coöperation and economics, for which K.F. furnished the literature. A Group may choose from among ten major subjects as follows: "Coöperation"; "The Production of Electric Lamps"; "The Problem of Monopolies"; "Coöperation and Agriculture"; "The Financial State of Societies"; "Cooperation and the Economic Life of the Nation"; "Control, Costs, and Expenses"; "Domestic Economy"; "The Housing Problem"; and "Topical Economic and Coöperative Problems." With each of these courses goes a special guidebook that suggests the general problem for study. K.F. also furnishes from its own flourishing editorial department other books bearing upon them along with specific pamphlets and most important of all, a series of questions for the Group to answer after reading and discussion. Each chapter of the guidebook is followed by three "Capital Questions." Answers to these questions are to be written out after a study meeting on the chapter has been held and the written answer sent to K.F.'s editorial department for correction.

The rule for the price policy of the Coöperative Movement usually is that the societies shall keep "common market prices." However, as the consumers' societies are not interested in keeping unfair prices—"common" or not—this rule is very indistinct in its formulation. It must be regarded from an historical point of view, if the true intention is to be correctly understood.

The problem of price policy is so important, and so often misunderstood, that it is necessary to deal thoroughly with this question. We start by reading . . . [here books and pamphlets, with page references, are cited] and discuss first the reasons why the societies shall not sell at their own cost price. Further, we must examine into the advantages and disadvantages of a *passive price policy,* the societies following the price of the private traders, and finally we will discuss the advantages and disadvantages of an active price policy, the societies trying to reduce the common price level.*

The guidebook, as this shows, is written very simply, in almost primer form. The questions are likewise simple and direct. "Is free competition between private shopkeepers as strong now as it formerly was?" "Is it reasonable for a financially strong and well-managed society always to follow the prices of private trade?" "Is it wise for the societies to try to reduce prices to the fullest extent rather than to create a surplus?" "Why are funds and dividends desirable?" Here is a capital question: "Which price policy should a strong coöperative society main-

* *Guide Book I: Coöperation,* chap. iv, "The Price Policy in the Coöperative Movement."

tain?" And here from the Group in Skalhamn is a "satisfactory" answer sent to K.F. for correction:

The price policy differs, depending upon different local circumstances and the financial position of the societies. For a newly established society it is usually important to keep "common market prices," as this results in the society's making a big surplus and being able to create reserve funds, and strengthen the financial position of the society. But there are instances when it cannot be considered reasonable to follow common market prices—our own society illustrates this fact. Had our society at the outset observed common market prices, the dividend could have been fixed at 15 or 20 per cent, and such a high dividend is for many reasons not suitable. When common market prices are so high, the society should from the beginning attempt to reduce prices, and such a price policy is a duty when the society has grown up to financial strength. In this way the consumers' organization is serving the interests of society as a whole, because the private shops are pressed to reduce their prices. From the propaganda point of view this price policy is preferable, too, because customers observe and appreciate attractive low prices. Such an active price policy is also a method of distributing wealth more equally, because it is in some degree diminishing the possibilities for creating privately owned capital and creating instead collectively owned capital.

The present direction of the movement is more or less clear. It can scarcely be said to be moving toward any sort of general collectivism. Rather, coöperative leaders seem to feel that the chief function of this remarkable organization of consumers, apart from a wholly distributive and productive one, is that of a brake to halt the excesses of capitalism; to prevent monopoly and the narrow concentration of wealth; in short to check the very tendencies by which capitalism tends to destroy itself. And in so far as the outsider may judge, the great mass of consumer members appear to be wholly in sympathy with this aim.

IV

LOW COST HOUSING

WHILE such analogies are of limited application, it is not far from the truth to say that Sweden twenty years ago was in the position that the United States now occupies with regard to mass housing. There was above all the realization that private business could not provide housing for the lowest income groups on the ordinary basis of private profit. Fifty years of agitation for slum clearance and better housing conditions had made that quite clear. This was the beginning of wisdom and eventually of a program that has resulted in large-scale building in Stockholm, Gothenburg, Malmö, and other cities. It has been said that Sweden is without slums, either in the city or the country, and while this may be over-generous, that ideal has certainly been approximated.

In Sweden those who were interested in promoting better housing had also come to the realization two decades or more ago that there would be little real progress until the interest of the group to benefit from improved housing was enlisted. And this, it may be noted here, is at the root of most of the reforms that Sweden has adopted; they are *sui generis,* growing out of a social need that has been keenly felt and insistently presented against a broad background of social and economic education; they have not, in short, been superimposed from above through the beneficence or the righteousness of a class that took its own superiority for granted. This is a vital distinction and it has led in Sweden more often than not to the coöperative solution of social and economic problems.

It is the coöperative method, together with assistance from the state in a variety of ways, that has made low-cost housing possible in Sweden. A housing shortage that existed before the outbreak of the World War was made acute by an influx of noncombatants who sought refuge in Stockholm. Every garret, every cellar, was occupied. The threat of the slums, as a breeder of crime, disease, and social decay, was very real. Numerous remedies had been tried—philanthropic building projects of one sort and another, municipal lodging houses and municipal farms for the poor—but they had all proved to be temporary expedients or worse. Rents at the close of the war were outrageously high in all the larger cities. Real estate interests were combined in what was in effect a housing trust.

In 1916 the Stockholm Coöperative Housing Society was organized, sponsored by the Central Labor Union, a powerful force in the political and economic life of the country. It was the first time that prospective tenants themselves, who made up the new organization, had the right to determine what kind of housing they would have. Six years later the society had proved its worth by tangible accomplishments in the shape of a half dozen coöperative apartment houses. A national organization, the Tenants Savings Bank and Building Society, was formed. In Swedish this is the Hyresgästernas Sparkassa och Byggnads-förening, ordinarily referred to as H.S.B.

H.S.B. has had a remarkable growth, and particularly in Stockholm. In that city of more than 600,000 population, at least 15 per cent of all families live in coöperative apartment houses. Building has continued throughout the depression, the construction program being carefully planned and financed several years in advance, through 1938. As with coöperation in other fields, H.S.B. has competed in the open market. Members have been attracted by the fact that the coöperative apartment houses are superior to others in almost every respect, besides being lower in price. They are designed for light, air, convenience and privacy, the newer units being in the functional style adopted by younger Swedish architects. The older buildings are somewhat more conservative in exterior design.

One man, Sven Wallander, has played an important part in the success of H.S.B. He combines remarkable skill and inventiveness as an architect with a keen business sense and a capacity for organization. But although Wallander has been perhaps the chief factor in the achievement of H.S.B., it has long since passed beyond the stage of dependence upon one individual.

H.S.B. builds its apartment houses on three different budgetary levels. The first type is known as the A-house. The householder who applies, as a member of H.S.B., for a coöperative apartment in an A-house must pay down 10 per cent of the cost of his apartment. This deposit varies from approximately $190 to $270 for an apartment of one room, bath, and kitchen. For five rooms, bath, and kitchen, the required deposit is from $1070 to $1180. Rents in the A-houses vary from $125 to $215 a year for the smallest apartments and from $700 to $865 for the largest.

In the B-houses the coöperator must pay down a 5 per cent deposit, ranging from $80 to $135 for the smallest apartments and from $350 to $400 for the largest. Rents for B-house apartments range from a minimum of $120 to a maximum of $485 for a five-room apartment. Obviously the A- and B-type houses are not for the lowest income group.

Prospective tenants for the C-houses pay no deposit at all. This is because the state and city provide virtually the entire capital for this type of coöperative apartment. In constructing the A-type, members furnish through their deposits 10 per cent of the capital, private banks and insurance companies another 10 to 15 per cent and the city and state 75 to 80 per cent. For the B-type the members' deposits represent but 5 per cent of the necessary capital, and the city and the central government contribute correspondingly more, that is 80 to 85 per cent. While the C-type are organized on a coöperative basis by H.S.B., they are really built by the city and all member tenants must be approved by city authorities.

Initial deposits made by future tenants are treated just as is capital from other sources. Member tenants receive 4 per cent interest annually on this deposit. They may receive this in cash each year, or they may receive 3 per cent in cash, the other 1 per cent being the premium on a special kind of insurance which provides that on the death of the head of the household the entire deposit is returned to the family and the annual rent is reduced by 20 per cent. Or a member tenant may allow his interest to accumulate and be compounded to the end of a twenty-year period.

The $200 collected as yearly rent for a B-house apartment would be charged off to the following operating and financial costs:

Interest on loans	$120.00
Amortizing loans	35.00
Service	21.00
Heat and hot water	16.00
Repairs	6.50
Reserve funds	1.50
	———
TOTAL	$200.00

At the end of the twenty-year period all deposits are returned in full, and annual rentals are automatically decreased by 20 per cent. The balance of the rent, 80 per cent, goes almost entirely to pay the cost of the actual upkeep and repair of the building. In addition to the deposit, member tenants in A- and B-type apartment houses are required to buy one share of stock in H.S.B. at $15 a share, drawing 4 per cent interest. This is still another source of capital.

Each separate apartment house is a unit, affiliated with the central organization, H.S.B., in much the same way that the retail store societies are affiliated with the Coöperative Union. And in the same way the various units control H.S.B., electing the members of the board of trustees that governs the central organization. Tenant members in a coöperative apartment house form their own organization on democratic lines, electing committees responsible for the management of the house, its cleanliness, the attractiveness of the gardens that surround it and the well-being of the members in general. There is a genuine group interest which focuses attention upon the collective management of the house and insures that members carry out the duties which have been delegated to them. In drawing the analogy with the Coöperative Union, it is interesting to note that almost every large coöperative apartment house has its own coöperative store, each one a unit of the Stockholm society.

More recently H.S.B. has been building still another type of coöperative apartment, the D-type house. These houses are intended for families with at least three children. They are financed by loans from the state, varying from 55 to 95 per cent of the value of the property. Furthermore, the state also subsidizes the rents of tenants in the D-type houses as follows: for families having three children up to 30 per cent; four children up to 40 per cent; and five children or more 50 per cent. The construction of these houses has been very largely put into the hands of special societies with a board of directors made up of three representatives of H.S.B. and two from the municipality. H.S.B., that is, the national organization, furnishes 5 per cent of the total capital required. Thus far these new houses have worked out extremely well with delinquencies in rent being practically nonexistent.

Planners and designers have done much to take the curse of bigness off the large apartment houses built by H.S.B., called familiarly "elephant" houses. To begin with they have been very carefully placed so that almost every window would command a pleasant outlook, of water or trees or a vista across the city. Two of the newest and largest houses are situated on a high bluff that commands a magnificent view of the city of Stockholm. There are balconies admirably planned for privacy and usually embellished with growing plants. Outer doorways are approached along garden pathways and borders of flowering shrubs. In the interior walls heavy insulation has been employed in an effort to make the apartments as nearly sound proof as possible.

There are many coöperative advantages at the disposal of all the member tenants of an H.S.B. house. Coöperative laundries are equipped with the most modern washing machines and mangles. Each woman who desires it is assigned a laundry period by the committee in charge of the laundry. The cost of power for the machines and gas for the mangles and special drying racks is a part of the general cost of the maintenance of the apartment building, and is prorated among all the member tenants. In a small separate building is a device which automatically beats rugs and mattresses and disposes of the dust.

The newer apartments are of cement and are therefore, of course, fireproof. Incinerator shafts on each landing convey garbage and trash to the basement where it is burned. The windows are made of so-called mirror glass, in one piece so that the view will not be obstructed. When the window must be washed, it is swung into the room. All of the floors are fitted with linoleum and this, too, simplifies the housekeeper's task. In every apartment there is a device into which a radio receiving set may be plugged to connect with a central radio that redistributes a variety of programs to the various flats. Incidentally, it is a house rule that each new tenant must have his possessions disinfected before he moves in so that there will be no danger of vermin. Provision for sun-bathing is made on the roofs of the houses.

Most remarkable of all are the coöperative nurseries in each apartment. Usually in a separate building in the near-by garden, they are done in soft colors, often with charming decorative detail. Here mothers may leave their children, in charge of nursery school attendants, from 6:30 in the morning to 6:30 in the evening, for a small sum each day. Even small babies may be left at the nursery, assured of the most scrupulous care. Children are put, at the first sign of illness, in a small infirmary in connection with each nursery. Ample play equipment and open air play spaces provide activity for the older youngsters. Adult groups in many apartment houses convert a part of the nursery into a gymnasium in the evening. H.S.B. has recently started a special school for training kindergarten teachers under the direction of Mrs. Alva Myrdal.

H.S.B., the central society, effects important savings for each house through wholesale purchases of coal and other supplies. In many ways the central organization looks after the welfare of the societies that control it. H.S.B. architects have designed handsome modern furniture perfectly adapted to flats of various sizes. This furniture is moderate in cost and may be purchased on most favorable terms. A tactful effort is made to induce tenant members to buy H.S.B. furniture rather than ill-adapted "suites" out of the department store. As a part of the propaganda for good, simple things, H.S.B. has organized several exhibitions of model apartments in Stockholm's Town Hall. They are done in furniture of excellent line, essentially simple and yet distinguished in treatment, usually of Swedish birch and other native woods. The walls are finished in soft shades and the practical sense of the Swedes is appealed to by an effective demonstration of the fact that light colored walls mean a saving in electricity, since dark walls make it necessary to use lamps of higher power. And exhibitions of apartments attractively decorated are held in all apartment houses for several weeks before the tenant members move in.

Coöperative apartment houses built in 1934 and 1935 were of the A- and B-type. More recently the Riksdag made available a generous appropriation for construction of low-cost apartments of the C-type, to be assigned to householders in the lowest income groups who have large families. This special consideration for families with children has come out of a deep concern over the declining birth rate, one of the lowest in the world. Of present tenant members now occupying coöperative apartment houses, 60.42 per cent are workers, 9.89 per cent are minor officials in public and private service, 23.84 per cent are clerks in stores and offices, and 5.85 per cent are higher officials, teachers, engineers, architects, and persons in other professions.

The latest statistics show what extraordinary progress H.S.B. has made in less than fifteen years. Throughout Sweden there are coöperative houses containing more than 30,000 flats and this, it must be recalled, in a country which is preponderantly rural. In Stockholm alone there are seventy-eight H.S.B. apartment houses in which some 70,000 people live. About $90,000,-000 has been spent on low-cost housing, by the state and its political subdivisions and through coöperatives such as H.S.B. This is nearly $15 for every man, woman, and child in the country. A comparable expenditure in the United States would be nearly two billion dollars, and that for urban housing alone.

H.S.B. is not the only coöperative housing organization in Sweden. Another architect who also combines great talent in his profession with broad social vision, Sven Markelius, has designed an apartment house in which the tenant members live on an even more coöperative basis than in the H.S.B. houses. In this new apartment house a coöperative kitchen supplies food to tenants in the fifty-seven apartments; coöperative servants take care of the apartments daily; children of tenant members may be kept by the day or through the entire twenty-four hours in a coöperative nursery.

Primarily Markelius designed the house for families in which both husband and wife are employed. In Stockholm, according to the 1930 census, 25.1 per cent of all married women are professional workers. No one, Markelius felt, had considered their real needs and desires in housing. Their entrance into professional and business life having occurred during the past two decades, they were compelled to adjust a career to the old style of living, frequently assuming the burden of both household and job. Markelius' Kollektivhus was designed to relieve the working wife and mother of all household responsibilities and at a cost within reach of families with relatively small incomes.

Returning from her job, as a typist, say, the housewife consults the menu of the day sent up from the coöperative kitchen. She and her husband and their two children may have their meal sent to their apartment by dumb-waiter or they may go down to the public dining room. Because it is a public dining room, serving excellent food, it is possible to have a rather wide choice of food. Having rested a little, she may send down to the nursery for her children. The cost by the day for their care is about one krona, that is approximately twenty-five cents in terms of current exchange, and they are under the care of trained child specialists. It is possible that if the apartment is small, the children may go back to the nursery for the night, at a very slight additional cost. Likewise older children are under the supervision of trained adults when they return from school and they, too, may sleep in the special children's quarters rather than in the family apartment.

The apartments, most of them small units, are designed with a great deal of flexibility so that by the use of screens, curtains, and couches that open into beds every possible advantage may be taken of all available space. There are also one-room apartments for single men and women. All apartments, except the one-room units, have kitchenettes, equipped with gas stove and refrigerator, where the tenant may prepare meals if she so prefers. The interiors, in the modern style, are very pleasant, particularly the restaurant and bar and the nursery. On the roof is a landscaped terrace for sun-bathing with a shower room.

Kollektivhus, completed in 1935, was opened with an unusual exhibition, leading architects and decorators being invited to decorate apartments for typical families chosen by Markelius and his associates. Thus one apartment was designed for a telephone worker, his wife, a fitter in a Stockholm dress shop, and their two children. The designer knew everything about this family before he planned the apartment, their income, how they would live, their tastes. And the visitor to the exhibit saw not only the completed apartment but photographs of the family in the apartment, as it would be lived in.

Kollektivhus was financed on much the same plan as the H.S.B. apartment houses. It cost about $250,000 which included the cost of the site. Approximately a tenth of this was advanced by the government, and prospective tenant members put up another tenth. A part of the balance was furnished by the banks and by ordinary credit sources. The remainder was advanced by the contractor. For the smallest flat, one room, balcony and bath, the down payment is 612 kronor, about $165, and the annual rent is $135. For the largest apartments, the equivalent of three or four rooms, kitchenette, bath, and balcony, the down payment is about $450 and the annual rental $350. In a sense Kollektivhus is an experiment. But the enthusiasm with which it has been received makes it seem probable that other similar units will be built.

The Coöperative Union has built one community of coöperative houses, for the employees of the Three Crowns flour mill. This colony is beautifully situated on a wooded hillside overlooking the water. Rows of single-family houses are built upon terraces in such a way that each row commands an unbroken view of woods and water. On the highest terrace is a three story apartment building. This is a logical corollary of the activities of the Union, and other similar communities will doubtless grow up about K.F.'s newer industries.

Quite apart from the central government and the coöperatives, the city of Stockholm has made its own frontal attack upon the housing problem and with a large measure of success. With a foresight that seems little short of amazing, the city in

1904 began to buy up large tracts of land near the city limits. This was before the expansion that followed upon the development of new industries and the boom that came during the war. Land prices were not high. Up to the present time the city has acquired about 20,000 acres located within a radius of nine miles from the center of the town. The total cost involved in these land purchases has been about $6,000,000.

As the city grew increasingly crowded, one excellent use was found for the land. Stockholm's Colony Gardens were developed on tracts owned by the city. These gardens illustrate very well the effort that has been made in Sweden to strike a balance between the past and the present; between a rural or semirural existence in which virtually the entire population was engaged in producing the immediate necessities of life and the modern, industrial world in which the things that men produce are remote from both their conception and their own immediate ability. Small garden plots were assigned, for little or no rent, to workingmen who lived in crowded city tenements. Here they could spend their Sundays or the long, light evenings in summer, raising flowers and vegetables.

The whole family came to luxuriate in the air and space of the country, and dig in the earth. Miniature houses were built on these plots to safeguard tools and garden supplies or to shelter the gardener and his family in the face of a sudden storm. In that splendid novel, *Our Daily Bread,* Gösta Larsson has shown how much the Colony Gardens meant to Swedish workers. They provided an interval of peace and quiet; but, more than that, a sense of independence and achievement that a man could not get from a machine, went with these garden plots.

They were in a sense a preparation for the "Magic House" project that Stockholm started in 1926. The city's "Magic House" has lived up to its name. It is a pre-fabricated house sold on the basis of the cost of the materials, and assembled with the labor of the purchaser. In less than ten years the "Magic House" plan has provided comfortable suburban homes for more than 15,000 people, and at a lower cost than almost any other housing scheme in Europe.

The prospective purchaser of one of the city's "Magic

Houses" goes to the Small House Bureau in the Town Hall and there fills out a lengthy application blank. His name will be put upon a waiting list, for "Magic Houses" are so desirable that the bureau is able to choose from the list those who will obtain the greatest good from moving from crowded districts of the city to the suburbs. Each applicant is investigated and first preference is given to families with children. Factory workers and others with jobs that keep them indoors are also in a preferred class. Again preference is shown to families whose income is within a range of $800 to $1300 a year. And since actual construction of the "Magic House" must be done in considerable part by the purchaser, those who are old or infirm are ruled out. Because it has always been possible to choose from a long list of applicants, the city has obtained a more or less homogeneous group of families with small incomes and relatively steady employment.

About 60 per cent of "Magic House" owners, as the following table shows, are engaged in indoor work:

Common laborers	3.6
Other laborers	22.7
Construction workers	23.1
Industrial workers	16.0
Railroad and street car workers	11.0
Business employees	2.7
Artisans	6.0
Foremen	2.7
Military	.2
Civil service employees	11.8
Unspecified	.2
TOTAL	100.0

The down payment for a "Magic House" is $80, and the prospective owner contributes through his own labor in the erection of the house about $270, which is about half of the total labor cost. He does not buy his lot; instead he leases it from the city for sixty years, with the option, under certain conditions, of renewing the lease should the city have no other plans for the use of the land. If the lease is terminated at the end of the sixty-year term, the city must redeem all improvements at a fair valuation. The lease may be transferred to legal heirs in the event of the owner's death and in other respects, too, it is more binding than an ordinary contract.

For his lot the home owner pays an annual rental of about 5 per cent of the value of the land. At present, this rental varies between slightly less than one cent and three cents, the average being about one and two-tenths cents, a square foot a year, depending upon the location and the price paid by the city for the land. Because these are not subsistence homesteads, in the sense that the owner must raise produce to augment his cash income, the average lot is only of ordinary size, sufficient for a house, vegetable and flower garden, and small lawn. The usual size for the larger type of residence is about 7,500 square feet and for the small houses the size of the lot ranges from 4,200 to 6,000 square feet. The city has provided large tracts for public parks, playgrounds, and swimming pools, apportioning the land so judiciously that each area is provided with recreation spaces conveniently at hand.

The "Magic House" plan was not adopted until after several other housing schemes had proved unsuccessful. First the city arranged to have private contractors build suburban houses on city-owned land, on the basis of a 25 per cent down payment, the balance in a loan guaranteed by the city. It was soon obvious that the income group most in need of housing could not possibly manage the 25 per cent down payment, and the city began to cast about for another scheme. As it first took shape, the new plan was to build the most rudimentary kind of small houses equipped with few modern conveniences. But a survey made by housing experts for the city of the so-called "jungle suburbs" surrounding other European capitals caused a complete change in this plan. The "Magic House," the city decided, should contain every modern convenience, including electricity, bath, toilet, central heating system, gas stove, sewer connection, and city water. It was to be a "Magic House" not only in the swift facility with which it would go up but in the ease of living which the occupants of the finished house would enjoy.

When the city has received the initial down payment of $80

Note: The photographs for the illustrations in this section were generously supplied by the American-Swedish News Exchange. Grateful acknowledgment is hereby made.

Above: Luma lightbulb factory, Stockholm. Owned and operated by the Swedish Coöperative Union and Wholesale Society.
Below: Coöperative Tre Kronor (Three Crowns) flour mill, situated on an island at the entrance to Stockholm's harbor.

Above: Coöperative department store, Ljusdal.
Below: Interior of coöperative supermarket, Stockholm.

Above: "Elephant" (apartment) houses in suburban Hässelby Strand district, west of Stockholm. *Below:* Civic center of Vällingby, one of the new self-contained suburbs on the outskirts of Stockholm.

Above: Slottsstadens coeducational high school in Malmö.
Below: Public school in Vällingby being decorated by artists.

Worker's house at the
Kosta Glassworks.

Old people's home,
Sabbatsberg, Stockholm.

H. M. King Gustaf VI Adolf of Sweden.

Modern housing development in Stockholm.

Above: The State Normal College in Stockholm. In the background: tower of the Stockholm stadium, built for the Olympic Games in 1912.
Below: Homes for workers at Gustavsberg coöperative ceramic factory.

from the prospective home owner, there is established in his favor by the city a credit account sufficient to cover the cost of materials above the amount of his cash payment. The amount of this credit varies, of course, according to the type of house selected and it may be paid off in annual installments over a period of thirty years. As security for this loan, the city takes a first mortgage on the house. Included in the amount that the home owner pays on this thirty-year basis is the cost to the city of administration, of instructors who give assistance in the erection of the houses and other overhead charges. Thus the taxpayer in Stockholm does not contribute in any manner whatsoever to this housing scheme, nor is the home owner in any way subsidized by the city.

Actually the credit granted by the city represents about 90 per cent of the estimated cost of the home. Most of the remaining 10 per cent is represented by the value of the labor contributed by the home owner. Throughout the construction period the city exercises the strictest supervision over the way in which the home builder uses the credit he has been granted. For, of course, the value of the city's mortgage on the property depends upon the quality of construction and the elimination of waste in materials and labor. If the entire credit is not used, the city sometimes allows the builder to make additions that naturally add to the value of the house. Sixty per cent of the homes have garages, for example, and in many instances glassed-in sun porches have been added. Often through the special skill of the builder a substantial saving on labor costs makes additional improvements possible.

When the contract is finally signed, there is tremendous excitement in the family of the prospective home owner. They have selected their lot and soon the materials for their house will be delivered, and it is up to them to build it. Early and late the whole family works, and brothers and cousins and uncles volunteer their services, somewhat after the fashion of a middle-western barn-raising. First the cellar must be dug, following the careful instructions contained in the handbook provided by the city. If difficulties, such as rock requiring blasting, are encountered, the city takes over and prorates the added cost among all the houses, so that no one individual is penalized.

When the excavation is completed, the aërated blocks for construction of the basement wall are delivered and the prospective householder turns mason, under the supervision of inspectors employed by the city. Because the basement is used for food storage, bathroom, laundry, workroom, and garage, great care is taken in waterproofing the foundation.

On every side "Magic Houses" are going up The head of the household comes direct from his work to the site of the new house. The older children may be there already, prepared to help or merely to become acquainted with the new neighborhood. In the late afternoon the wife arrives with a hamper of lunch and the whole family has a picnic supper on the site where the house will rise. Nearby are other similar groups, and children and grownups strike up early friendships with future neighbors.

The joists and the flooring arrive from the factory all cut to exact size and numbered in accord with the detailed plan that the householder must follow. When the foundation work is completed, the ready-made wooden wall sections are installed and here expert workmen are usually required. Experts are needed in most instances, too, for the installation of electric wiring, water pipes, and plumbing fixtures and to do the sheet-iron and glazing work. As the work progresses through the summer and early fall, numerous small tasks fall to the lot of the children. The wife, too, does her share, with a paintbrush or even a hammer and a saw. At last the head of the household is on top of the roof laying the tiles. The weather stripping is all in place. The instructor, who has checked up on every detail as construction has gone forward, will come only once more. The kitchen cabinet, closet, and shelves, all finished at the factory, have been installed and a housewarming is close at hand. The "Magic House" has taken shape in a few short months under the eyes of the family that will occupy it.

If it is a house of Type No. 1, it contains in the basement a bath and toilet, laundry equipment, two closets for food storage, furnace, and coal bin; on the first floor are a hall, kitchen, and living room; and on the second floor, hall, closet, and large bedroom. In the next size, Type No. 2, the basement has in addition a garage or workshop of generous proportions; there are a dining room and living room on the first floor, and the second floor has two bedrooms. The most popular is type No. 6, containing three rooms, kitchen, and lavatory.

The saving effected by installing the bathroom fixtures in the basement is sufficient to justify this minor inconvenience. These are not, it must be remembered, in any sense jerry-built houses. They are made to stand the rigors of a severe northern winter. When they are completed, they comply in every respect with Stockholm's strict building laws.

Proof of the success of the plan is the fact that during the depression the city, while forced to take back a few houses, suffered no loss. Axel Dahlberg, director of the Real Estate Department of the City of Stockholm, has been very active in developing the "Magic House" plan since it started and he has without doubt had a great deal to do with the rapid growth of the scheme. The activities of the Small House Bureau, within the Real Estate Department, are kept out of politics and are not affected by changing administrations since employees are chosen by the merit system.

The city authorities make it plain to the householder that he must meet his financial obligations each month just as though he were dealing with a private firm. Perhaps because the investigation of prospective home owners has been so thorough, the city's losses have been negligible. For 1934 the Real Estate Department of the City of Stockholm reported a surplus of 817,000 kronor on its operations which went into the city's general surplus for that year, amounting to a total of 13,500,-000 kronor.

Any one who has seen the handsome, scrubbed cottages of Dalecarlia, the clean, modern homes of the miners at Kiruna, or the tiny waterside villas built by the workingmen of Stockholm on all the islands of the archipelago must realize that the Swedes have a special capacity for home making and home ownership. There has been this to build on in any housing program, coöperative or state.

V

THE STATE IN INDUSTRY

STATE ownership is deeply rooted in the Swedish past. It is at the heart of what has been for many years Sweden's principal business—forestry and the industries that are built upon wood and wood derivatives. Long before wood pulp became an important factor in world trade, the state had its own forest lands. With ownership went a popular sense of responsibility for preserving a fundamental source of national wealth. This early responsibility has developed for more than a century and a half, evolving into a conservation program designed to perpetuate a system of forests which will produce a constant yield of timber.

The beginning of conservation was in 1600 when the first national forest law was passed. Ever since that time the state has been strengthening the terms of its guardianship over the forests. Likewise the paper industry, which eventually was to draw upon forest resources, had an early development, dating back to the sixteenth century when the Klippan Paper Mill, still in existence, was built. With the introduction of the steam sawmill, there was opened up in the province of Norrland the most extensive, continuous area of woodland in Europe outside of northern Russia.

The Swedish timber industry has grown to a place of primary importance, not only for Sweden but for Europe. Great Britain has been the leading customer ever since the duty on timber was reduced in 1821, and when this duty was abolished in 1866, a large share of Sweden's wood products went to England. After the World War Sweden benefited from the decline in the Russian timber industry and succeeded in supplying an even larger portion of the English demand.

Lumbering has long provided Swedish farmers with a source of cash income to augment the returns from farms that are none too fertile. Forest skills are passed on from generation to generation and in the slack season on the farm scarcely a household but supplies one or more workers. They bring their own horses and are ordinarily employed on a piece-work basis. Labor employed thus year after year makes for careful and intelligent use of forest lands and for stability and permanence in an industry that is elsewhere notoriously unstable.

Such is the condition prevailing, too, in the towns that have grown up around the sawmills and wood-pulp factories. Agnes Rothery has given a delightful description of one of these sawmill towns, Jervsöbaden, as unlike what we in America understand by the phrase "sawmill town" as anything could well be. This small, immaculate community, where life runs along such a pleasant and well-ordered course, and many others like it have been for years the basis of Sweden's industry in wood.

Training in forestry methods and propaganda for conservation also got an early start. The State College of Forestry was founded in 1828, the Swedish Institute of Experimental Forestry in 1902. And besides these there are fifty-five state forestry schools in different sections of the country. While there have been local laws restricting the right of the owner to dispose of his timber since the middle of the fifteenth century, it was not until 1905 that a general law was passed requiring that all timber cut be replaced within a reasonable length of time. Another law was passed in 1923 stipulating that all forest ground be used for the production of timber and prohibiting any of it lying bare or being too sparsely planted. The private owner has the strongest incentive to safeguard his property, one section of the law requiring him to reforest if the original timber is destroyed by fire, pests, storms, or other accidents. There are special laws regarding "protective forests" at the timber line in the mountainous areas at the north and similar special laws favoring forests along the seacoast which are difficult to regenerate.

The state husbands its own forest lands so skilfully and thriftily that they serve as a model for private owners. It was in 1752 that the national government began a general survey and reallotment of all land. Largely as a result of this survey the state acquired the bulk of the 10,793,900 acres of forest that it now owns. The total land area of the country, it must be remembered, is 102,000,000 acres, of which more than half is in forest. Besides the forest area that it owns outright the state administers 741,000 acres belonging to the state church and 1,976,000 acres owned by the municipalities. Of the balance of Sweden's forests, by far the greater part is in small farm holdings. Private corporations, most of them in the wood-pulp industry, own 15,511,600 acres.

These private companies are not allowed under the law to increase their acreage by purchase from other classes of owners. In contrast, the state is slowly adding to its holdings, particularly in the south, where the most profitable forest areas are found. The primary aim is to build up tracts large enough to form independent units for profitable forestry by state foresters. Small wooded estates have been acquired only when they have adjoined other state forest lands. These purchases have been made for the most part with funds from the sale of small farms that have belonged to the state. A great deal of the government's timber is in the north, situated in the interior and in the higher mountain areas where it is of slight value at present.

In the lumber business the state competes on equal terms with private companies. On the amount of its gross income the state pays local taxes to the various provinces in which the forests are situated, as well as the general tax to the central government. Together these amount to about 10 per cent of the gross income from the state forests. To take two prosperous years, before the wood-pulp industry was affected by the world-wide depression, the state forests yielded in 1926 a profit of approximately $3,024,000 and in 1928 a profit of $4,320,000.

The Board of Crown Lands and Forests in Stockholm administers the state forests with the objective of realizing each year an amount of revenue commensurate with conservative methods of forestry. District foresters, trained in the special forestry schools that are distributed throughout Sweden, are directly in charge of the work in each of 600 districts. The forester follows a working schedule laid down by the board but this schedule allows considerable latitude for the judgment of the individual official. Similarly the big private companies have put their forests in charge of trained foresters who direct all operations. And the state foresters keep a watchful eye on private operators. Under their direction ditches are dug, brooks cleaned, logging sites inspected and millions of spruce and pine seedlings sent out from propagating stations to be set out in public and private areas.

Although the state is in the timber business in competition with private capital, on an equal basis with no special favors asked or granted, the government has not entered into direct competition with private mining corporations. At one time the state owned the largest iron ore deposits in the country, in Lapland. The story of how the state surrendered these deposits and subsequently reasserted its claim to this fabulous wealth in the far north is interesting for the light that it throws on the relationship between government and business.

According to mining laws that go a long way back, the prospector who finds a deposit of ore has a right to claim it, with the reservation that the owner is entitled to one half of all royalties realized from the exploitation of the ore. From the beginning of time almost, the state owned the land around the town of Kiruna, not far from the northern boundary of Sweden. But in order to encourage prospecting the state surrendered its prior right as owner, and in this way lost the enormously rich iron mountains, Kirunavaara and Luossavaara, the full value of which became apparent only as industry developed.

These great deposits of iron, perhaps the richest in the world, were under control of a private company. There was, however, no railroad line between Kiruna and the nearest port, and when the company applied for the right to build such a line, the state said no. The state itself built the line and in a contract with the company specified that 1,200,000 tons of ore a year should be transported on this state-owned railway.

Later on, the company owning the mines at Kiruna was acquired by the Grängesberg-Oxelösund Company, one of the largest industrial corporations in the country, and still another firm was formed to exploit these iron mines—Luossavaara-Kirunavaara Aktiebolaget, usually shortened to L.K.A.B. When foreign capital threatened to gain control of this firm, there was an appeal to the state for the right to increase the amount of ore carried over the state's railroad. And it was at this point that the state used its rail monopoly to regain at least some degree of control over the iron mountains.

The government, a conservative government, replied to the company: We cannot grant your request unless you agree to surrender to the state one half of the shares of the company, and also to cede the right to take over the other half at a future date in return for a payment to be based on the average profit per ton during a ten-year period. Perforce the company agreed to this arrangement. The state in turn agreed to keep freight rates low and guaranteed the company against export duties. From time to time the company has had to make further requests to carry even more iron ore, and each time the state demanded new concessions.

Finally, in 1927, all the old contracts were canceled and a new one worked out. Under this contract the state has 50 per cent of the shares, the company 50 per cent; the state names four directors, the company four directors; but the managing director and president is named by the Grängesberg-Oxelösund Company, and it is his vote that is decisive in the event of a tie. Under the new contract the state must receive 1.50 kronor (37½ cents) a ton royalty on each ton mined whether there is a profit or not; after this has been met then a dividend may be paid on the Grängesberg shares equivalent to 1.50 a ton; and all profits thereafter are divided equally between state and company.

During the depression years it was necessary to make some adjustment in this arrangement, for it worked a severe hardship on the company. In the year ending September 30, 1932, for example, the company lost nearly $5,000,000 on its operations but nevertheless had to pay the state a royalty of $1,000,000 on the ore that was mined. Also under the 1927 contract the state's revenue from the railway line is guaranteed in a clause which provides that the company shall make up the difference if freight payments do not cover all costs, including amortization and interest at 5 per cent on the whole amount invested in the line.

Now, of course, with the armament boom, the company is returning a very large profit indeed, and payments which the state allowed the company to defer during the depression have long since been repaid. In 1947 and every tenth year after that the state will have the right to buy up the shares held by the company. The price of the shares will be based upon the average price for a ton of ore during the ten-year period.

Apparently the public is satisfied with this curious arrangement, this hybrid economic structure. It has met the test that the Swedes apply: Does it work? Naturally the businessmen who controlled the Grängesberg corporation were not very pleased by the state's invasion of the rich field they had acquired for themselves, but they have come to accept it as inevitable and they have made every effort to meet the requirements of the government.

It may be said here that this is typical of the attitude toward government competition. There has been no arbitrary rule of state ownership *per se*. When it has seemed advisable, for one reason or another, and when it has been wholly practical, the state has not hesitated to enter the field of industry. Always, it should be added, the state has been a competitor on equal footing, whether in a complex field or in a pursuit that is relatively simple and with a long history of public ownership, such as forestry.

Vast quantities of iron ore have passed over the railroad built by the state from the mines to Luleå, a port on the Baltic, and to Narvik, a Norwegian port. The return has been so great, despite the advantageous rate which the company obtained, that it was found possible to electrify the line linking the mines with the two ports. It is farther north than any other electric railway in the world, and the Swedes are proud that this is an achievement of their state.

Both provinces and municipalities levy high taxes against L.K.A.B. By means of these taxes model mining towns were created. There, far to the north, where in the middle of winter the sun scarcely rises at all, where there is at most an hour or two of daylight, one finds excellent public libraries, public baths and gymnasiums, and public lecture and concert halls. The workers' homes are all electrified, many of them heated by electricity and equipped with the latest labor-saving devices.

The eighteen hundred workmen at Kiruna are said to be the best paid industrial workers in Europe. The mines are ideally equipped to care for the health and comfort of the workman. When he arrives in the morning, having come on a street car on which he rides free of charge, or on his own bicycle or even in his motor car, the miner leaves his street clothes in a locker and puts on his work clothes. At the end of the day he takes a hot bath, a steam bath, and a cold bath as well as a sun bath under the ultra-violet lamp if he desires. It is no wonder that his wife is able to keep their house so immaculate. His children go to a free school where they receive free dental service and special attention and care for their health. Hot luncheons are served in the schools without charge. And they are good schools that provide besides a rudimentary scholastic background special training to equip a boy or a girl with a trade.

Because the iron and steel industry depended, directly or indirectly, in large part upon a flourishing world trade, it was here that the greatest volume of unemployment occurred at the depth of the depression. It was so great in fact that the community itself established a school in the south of Sweden to equip young men with special skills and help them to become established in other communities. The decline in the world demand for iron and steel was obviously quite beyond the power of the Swedish government to remedy. And yet, ran the argument of those who believe great care should be exercised in extending state ownership, this obvious fact would have been ignored had the state been engaged in direct operation of the mines; the decline in mining would have become a political issue and would have been met with an expedient political solution. This argument serves at least as a strong reminder that Sweden is a small country dependent upon foreign trade in a capitalist world.

The intelligent way in which Sweden is exploiting her latest treasure trove, the gold deposits in the Boliden mine at Västerbotten, not far from the Arctic Circle, illustrates very well the fixed policy toward basic natural resources. This important deposit, which contains, besides gold, silver, copper, arsenic, and other minerals, was discovered in 1924 by the most painstaking scientific methods, involving the use of electro-magnetism as a kind of modern divining rod. This was the climax of a search that had begun six years before in which the state participated with private interests.

The major deposit was found on a rocky, barren farm owned by a widow, Margareta Lundberg, who had been struggling for years to wrest a living from it. As a primary step, the Widow Lundberg was given a generous annuity. The first workmen at the site, miles from a town or railroad branch, had to live in camps. But roads were rapidly built and a railroad spur constructed to connect with the branch line from the Lapland main trunk to Skellefteå on the coast. It was extraordinary how rapidly an entire community came into being about the Boliden mine in the heart of wooded country close to the Arctic Circle. It was no pioneer shanty town. Kirunavaara and Gellivare served at the outset as the pattern which the builders followed, and so another model mining village came into being.

The ore was of a puzzling type that at first offered certain difficulties to metallurgists. It was necessary to build a special kind of smelter with what is said to be the tallest smokestack in Europe. The efforts of all who participated in the venture have been richly rewarded, particularly since the rise in the international gold price.

The dividend declared in 1933 was 15 per cent and in 1934 20 per cent. Of the net profits that year, amounting to 18,920,-000 kronor, roughly $5,000,000, only 8,400,000 kronor were distributed to stockholders. The rest went for taxes, sinking funds, various reserve funds and, above all, to a social welfare fund which is intended to provide for the workers and the community when the present ore deposit is exhausted. Because of the high price of gold, ore was worked in 1933 which contained a higher percentage of gold than the estimated average for the entire mine and, consequently, there was set aside for the sinking fund the sum of 4,900,000 kronor as compared with 2,750,-000 the year before. Thus it is computed that the entire value of the mine will be written off well in advance of its exhaustion, which according to engineers will be in 1955. The government has throughout exercised the closest supervision over the exploitation of the Boliden ore deposits, safeguarding the interests of the workers and the state.

In the same district there are numerous other ore deposits, located by both government and private prospectors. New methods of treating the reserve ore will make it possible, it is said, to exploit deposits that at present seem unprofitable. The great smelter at Skellefteå is so planned that it will serve as the focus for ore from a wide area. It merely happens that the Boliden deposit is the largest and most conveniently located find and therefore was exploited first.

The ordinary daily output in 1934 was between two and three bars of pure gold, each bar weighing twenty-seven and a half pounds. Total production in 1933 was 16,385 pounds. In contrast to world gold production, slightly less than 1,500,000 pounds in 1932, this seems negligible, scarcely 1 per cent of the total. But nevertheless Sweden is first in Europe in gold production, having taken the lead from Transylvania which has held it ever since the time of the Roman Empire, more than two thousand years ago. And the precious metal out of the Boliden mine has been a helpful factor in building up Sweden's gold reserves.

What is more important, skilful technicians have been able to extract from Boliden ore silver, copper, and sulphur in considerable amounts. About half of the silver now used in Sweden is of domestic production, whereas a few years ago almost the entire amount had to be imported. The Swedes take great pride in the fact that the commemorative five-kronor pieces minted in honor of the quincentenary of the Riksdag were of native silver and that many of the wedding gifts presented to Princess Ingrid and Crown Prince Frederik of Denmark were made of gold and silver from a Swedish mine.

To the practical advantage of industry the Boliden mine will produce about 6,000 tons of copper a year, one fifth of Swedish consumption. And while the world price of copper is low at present in view of a plentiful supply, this one fifth would be of primary importance in the event of another world war and consequent embargoes on world trade. Another industrial necessity out of Boliden, which Sweden has hitherto had to import, is sulphur. Already there is a potential capacity of 50,000 tons a year, about 70 per cent of the Swedish demand. Eventually, it is said, the entire demand for sulphur in its various forms can be met with ore from Boliden.

The attitude of the state toward the nation's basic resources has served as a foundation on which has been built the whole structure of state-owned industry, extending in recent decades into complex fields such as power production. How important this attitude has been in determining the success of the state's program it would be difficult to say, for it is impossible to appraise such imponderable factors. But undoubtedly the public point of view has been conditioned by the guardianship that the central government established long ago over the riches of the earth. It may be contrasted with the wild exploitation of American natural resources which the state, in a sense, aided and abetted. How deeply this has affected the American attitude toward the property of the Commonwealth, the public domain, has been painfully obvious. If only as a form of rudimentary social education, the ownership in Sweden of valuable forest lands has been immensely worth while. Since the government was able to compete successfully with private enterprise in the timber business, the public reasoned, the state might with considerable assurance of success undertake to build its own power system.

VI

A NATIONAL POWER SYSTEM

SWEDEN is richly endowed with swift rivers that are broken by magnificent falls, roaring and tumbling along narrow channels. From time immemorial these waterfalls, or a large number of them, have been owned by the state. And this was a factor of great importance when the government began to plan its own power system, a system which was to compete with private companies long established.

The development of the state power system is an excellent example of public planning on a realistic basis. It is a form of "planned economy," to use a dubious phrase, in which from the beginning the purpose and the direction were made perfectly clear. The state was to compete with private power companies in order to bring about lower rates and in order to prevent monopoly control of this modern necessity. From the first the state has aimed at a comprehensive system which should be the core of the nation's power production. And this objective has never been lost sight of, so that it is possible today not only to look back to the beginning in 1909 but to look ahead to developments that will take place in 1945.

There was created in 1909 a Water Power Administration, consisting of a central board of management, the Royal Board of Waterfalls, together with subordinate local administrations, authorized to develop a state power system. In the power field at that time there was intense competition. Under Swedish law monopoly franchise is never granted by the central government and only rarely by the municipalities which have jurisdiction within urban areas. Two or more companies could compete in the same district and with the field thus open to all comers it is not surprising that rivalry was bitter. A state concession to operate in a district means merely the right to erect poles and string power lines. Similarly, a franchise within the corporate limits of a city or town usually means only the right to use the streets for power facilities.

In the face of almost unrestricted competition the state was able to develop its own power resources, determined always to make power plants and power lines pay their own way. Because of the importance and the far-reaching significance of this venture, authority was carefully delegated between the central board and the local administrations. The Royal Board of Waterfalls was given a considerable measure of independence and among the members of the board were several men of long business and engineering experience, drawn from outside the government. The latter do not take an active part in management but are called upon to help in deciding issues involving general policy.

The largest responsibility falls upon the director general who is chairman of the board and chief of the administration and its staff and must therefore decide all major questions. But his job is facilitated by the fact that the work of the board is divided among five departments or bureaus, each one with certain delegated powers and responsibilities. The most important of the five divisions is the Power Department which has charge of the management and operation of the power plants together with the interconnecting transmission systems and as well directs the sale of power, besides taking part in the preparation of plans for new hydraulic and steam power plants.

The Royal Board of Waterfalls first began a thorough inventory of the water power resources of the country. The survey, conducted by the State Meteorological Hydrographical Office, which publishes the Register of Waterfalls, has thus far covered about 75 per cent of the water resources of the country. It has been estimated that about 32,500,000,000 annual kilowatt hours can be produced economically in Sweden. At present the state contributes about 35 per cent of all power produced. Of the total state production, more than 90 per cent is water power.

Briefly the development of the state's network may be traced here. At the heart of the system is the Central Block which feeds a populous and highly industrialized area in the middle of Sweden. The first unit in the Central Block, the Trollhättan power plant utilizing the falls of the Göta Älv, Sweden's largest river from the point of view of stream flow, was completed in 1910. The Trollhättan plant produces 127,000 kilowatts.

Five years later the state completed its second major power plant, Älvkarleby, equipped for 67,000 kilowatts, also a unit in the Central Block. For a reserve, when drought should reduce the power available from stream flow, the state next built the steam plant at Västerås. And hardly had that been completed when the Board of Waterfalls began to plan the hydroelectric development at Motala. Finally these three were linked by transmission lines for 77,000 volts and with the imperative demand for power created by the wartime boom, another trunk line was constructed between Trollhättan and Västerås. With this the nucleus of the Central Block was complete. A power station at Lilla Edet, utilizing the fall of the Göta Älv from the lowest level at Trollhättan to the sea, was added in 1926. In February of 1934 the Vargön plant was completed and the Malfors station was completed somewhat in advance of schedule and put into operation early in 1936.

The Central Block has at present a capacity of 270,000 kilowatts of water power which will be materially increased with the completion of stations now under construction. Through skilful social and technical planning the state has made the utmost use of the entire fall of the Göta River; a splendid natural resource put at the service of the whole people. In the evenness of the flow of water, attributable to the influence of Lake Vänern, and in the way in which the major falls occur, the Göta is almost ideally suited to power production on a large scale. Now the state is buying up riparian rights around Lake Vänern so that the water level, and therefore the power capacity of the river, can be more nearly controlled.

Within the province of Norrland are the two other state power blocks, Norrfors and Porjus, the latter extending far beyond the Arctic Circle close to the northernmost boundary of Sweden. Porjus, the older, came into being in 1915 in connection with the development of the great mines at Kiruna. The Porjus power plant can produce in a year of normal flow up to 500,000,000 kilowatt hours. The Norrfors hydroelectric plant, opened in 1926, together with the new Sillre power station, which is linked with it, can produce up to 200,000,000 kilowatt hours a year.

As the state became an effective competitor in the power field, there was a gradual, but nevertheless perceptible, downward movement of rates. For the most part the state has been a wholesaler of power. It sells to cities and towns which in turn sell at retail. Gothenburg, the second city, buys state power. Power from the state system is sold to the state railways, an important market. Coöperative societies in rural areas absorb a substantial volume of the state's production. And in competition with private companies the Royal Board of Waterfalls makes power contracts with large papermills, sawmills, mines, and electro-chemical and electro-thermal industries.

The state has followed the policy of selling its power at a low rate—representing the cost of production plus a modest margin of surplus. The power industry in Sweden, both public and private, has been rationalized on a basis of the national need for power, with state competition the controlling factor. This has been the effect of public enterprise in a country where utility "regulation," as it is understood elsewhere, is all but unknown.

Private and public power plants are in many instances linked together, both contributing to an adequate, unified transmission system serving a definite area. This kind of coöperation is difficult for the outsider, and especially the visitor from America, to understand. With regard to future development, there is an excellent illustration of how the state and private power interests have learned to coöperate since the end of the period of violent competition. A power line is to be constructed between Stadsforsen and Västerås in part to serve the railway line between Storvik and Ånge which is to be electrified by order of the Riksdag. The Royal Board of Waterfalls has arranged with a private electrical company to supply the railway with power until the state's new power line shall be completed. Similar agreements are not uncommon. It must be realized, of course, that this did not come about until the state had demonstrated that it was a force to be reckoned with.

One reason why the margin of surplus, "profit," from the

public power system is small is the fact that the state recognizes a social responsibility to extend power facilities into remote rural areas. Twenty-five years ago it was shown that it was practicable to extend power lines into these areas and the movement has continued ever since. During the World War, when fuel and illuminating oil were difficult to obtain, electrification was given a great impetus. This rapid development continued because of the flourishing condition of agriculture during the two years immediately following the war. Progress has been slower since 1920. At present about 50 per cent of the agricultural area of Sweden is electrified. In districts covered by state power systems about 60 per cent of the cultivated area has electricity.

Rural electrification in Sweden is accomplished almost entirely through coöperative societies made up of consumers of electric power. The individual society must provide its own capital to build a distributing system. Each member may subscribe a certain amount or the society may offer bonds in return for the necessary capital. In the latter event each consumer must pay his share of the interest and amortization. The average cost of the distributing networks, about 70 kronor, more than $18 per tariff unit, is comparatively high because so many were built at a time when metal prices were advanced. At prices which prevailed during the depression, the cost per tariff unit was about 40 kronor, or approximately $10.70.

This may be compared with the American practice in those few areas where societies for the coöperative distribution of electric power exist. Most societies in Washington and Idaho require the payment of an initial membership fee, $100 or $150, which may be paid, however, over a considerable period of time. At Rupert, Idaho, the membership fee is $100 and in addition each member of the society pays about $90 for the cost of transformer and wiring to the premises. The Ohop Valley Mutual Light and Power Company, at Eatonville, Washington, purchasing power from the municipal plant at Tacoma, has a membership fee of $210; this includes the cost of running a line to the home of the individual member and that amount must be paid at once in cash. The relative purchasing power of the krona and the dollar must be taken into account in these comparisons. The cost per tariff unit in Sweden prior to the depression, $18.50, would be roughly equivalent to a cost of somewhat more than $35 a tariff unit in this country.

Having accumulated sufficient capital, the society then proceeds to build a network which will carry power to all the members of the society. Here the society has the assistance of the Royal Board of Waterfalls which not only plans but later will control the network. Besides this the Board must approve the rates to be charged by the society and in the contract with the Board the society agrees to follow certain regulations which the Board shall lay down. Another service that the Board performs is to provide, free of charge, account books for the society, as well as necessary sets of forms. Experts sent out by the Board assist in calculating the annual budget and in closing the books. In short, the rôle of the Board is more or less paternalistic inasmuch as it takes every precaution to see that the coöperative power systems do not get into any kind of trouble, either technical or financial.

Having financed and built the network, the society is prepared to take power from state plants, generally at a tension of 3,300 volts. The network includes, besides the necessary local supply system, transformer stations for stepping the power down to low tension. The operation and upkeep of the local supply lines are the responsibility of the society.

Ready to operate, the society must make a choice between two different wholesale rates for power. One is the industrial rate and the other is the rural rate. The larger coöperative societies, especially those which have a considerable industrial outlet or have in their districts at least one fairly large settled community, find it to their advantage to take the industrial rate. Under this rate the average cost of a kilowatt hour of energy to the society in 1932 was 6.35 öre, or approximately one and three-fourths cents. The majority of societies take their power under the rural rate which in 1932 meant an average cost to the society per kilowatt hour of 7.35 öre, nearly two cents. The size of the coöperative power societies varies widely but on the average a society includes 2,000 tariff units and consumes about 130,000 kilowatt hours a year, with eighty kilowatts the maximum demand.

The rate paid by consumer members varies somewhat from society to society. But as a rule payments are fixed at 3.50 kronor a year for each share of stock in the society, plus eight to ten öre per kilowatt hour from January to April and from September to December, and four to five öre during the months from May to August inclusive. This does not include the charge which the society must assess to meet the first cost of building the local supply system. But if an individual member has already paid his full share of this cost, then there is no additional charge on his bill.

Electrification of Swedish households has developed to a remarkable degree. Here again the war, with the resultant scarcity of imported fuels, furnished a strong impetus. The system of rates that has been worked out in many communities has done a great deal to bring about a generous use of electricity. In most towns and villages special rates have been introduced by which current taken in excess of a certain number of kilowatt hours per room or square foot of floor space is supplied at a reduced price, ranging from six to ten öre, that is from about 1.6 cents to 2.7 cents. And even lower rates, phenomenally low rates, are found in many communities. The lowest rate is said to be that at Umeå, three öre, less than a cent, per kilowatt hour. The rate at Kiruna and Malmberget is almost as low, 150 kronor per kilowatt and year for basic power. These rates are exceptional but in many other instances power is supplied during special low tariff periods for water heating and similar purposes at from two to three öre per kilowatt hour.

The capitalization of the state power system for 1933 was put at 290,600,000 kronor, on which the Royal Board of Waterfalls realized an operating profit of 16,500,000 kronor, equivalent to a dividend of 5.68 per cent. For 1934 the capitalization was 295,200,000 kronor, the operating profit 17,600,000, and the dividend rate 5.95. A more detailed analysis of the 1932 figures is available. This shows a capitalization of 288,500,000 kronor and an operating profit of 15,720,000. But from the latter figure is deducted interest on the state's investment, at the actual state rate, 4.66 per cent, and interest on the as yet unexploited waterfalls, which have been the property of the state for many centuries, at 4 per cent. These two items of interest

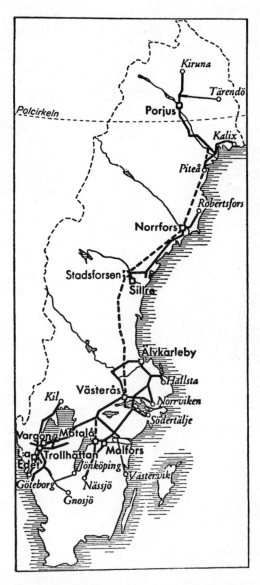

*Chart showing major transmission lines in the
government's power system, with dotted lines
indicating future construction*

total 14,642,000. Deducting these interest charges from the operating profit there remains a "net profit" of 1,078,000 kronor, about $280,000. For the two following years the "net profit" would be somewhat larger.

It is a small sum. But the system is not run for profit. The rates established by the state are predicated upon the cost of production plus just such a small margin. It should be noted, incidentally, that in arriving at this "profit" figure the state has followed strict accounting procedure, allowing a generous sum for the value of the waterfalls which cost nothing inasmuch as they have come down as a natural heritage.

It is estimated that by 1945 the available power from the Central Block will be fully utilized. Supplementary power required will then be taken from the River Indalsälven where the state owns important water resources. The first power station to be constructed on the Indalsälven, according to plans prepared by the Royal Board of Waterfalls, was that at Stadsforsen. The Riksdag approved construction of a transmission line linking the various units in the state power system, including the station to be built at Stadsforsen, in one unified whole. This line was ready for operation in the fall of 1937, extending from the Porjus system to the Norrfors plant, and from Norrfors, by way of the site on which the Stadsforsen station will be constructed, to Västerås. The accompanying diagram shows how well the system has been coördinated with the completion of the new line. The state power lines, linking together the great hydroelectric stations that the state has developed, extend for nearly a thousand miles, from one end of the country to the other.

Despite the success of the central government in the power field, many municipalities have developed their own plants. The City of Stockholm built a steam power plant in 1892, buying additional power of the state's Älvkarleby hydroelectric system from 1916 to 1919. In 1918 Stockholm built its own hydroelectric plant at Untra Falls on the Dalälven. Besides this the city owns two thirds of the shares in the private company that exploits the Lanfors Fall on the same river and in 1926 acquired outright a portion of that fall. Stockholm in 1934 realized a "profit" of 2,414,000 kronor from its power system and 988,000 from its municipal gas works.

It is not uncommon for a city to control or own a company which is only nominally a private company. Far to the north, the plant at Skellefteå is almost entirely owned by the municipality. I recall the intense pride with which the chief engineer related his triumph in obtaining a contract to supply the mines at Boliden with power over the competing bid of the Royal Board of Waterfalls. He was proud, too, of his model plant and its efficiency.

It is generally agreed in Sweden that W. Borgquist has contributed a great deal to the success of the state power system as director, during the past fifteen years, of the Royal Board of Waterfalls. Widely known for his achievement in Sweden, he has been called upon by Czechoslovakia, the Irish Free State, and other new countries to give advice in the establishment of state power systems. It is interesting to note, too, that when big business sought a man of high rank in the power field to lend his name and advice to a vast private enterprise Borgquist was singled out. Some years ago he was named chairman of the board of the L. M. Ericsson Company, manufacturers of telephones and electrical apparatus, one of the largest firms in the country. Instead of paying a titled nonentity to serve as "window dressing," as might easily have happened in England, for example, the Ericsson Company obtained not only the prestige of Borgquist's name but his immense knowledge of power development.

Largely because of the success of the state's power program it has been possible to electrify many hundreds of miles of railroad owned and operated by the government. In fact, except for certain small private railway companies, only state lines have thus far been converted to electric power. Electrification was begun on the line that transports iron ore from Kiruna to the Norwegian border, a distance of about eighty miles. This was completed in 1915, and eventually the line from Kiruna to Luleå was also electrified, making a total of about 280 miles, part of it well beyond the Arctic Circle.

Conversion of the line from Stockholm to Gothenburg, perhaps the most important route in the country, was completed in 1926, a total of approximately 285 miles. And in the midst of the depression the state initiated and carried through the electrification of about 530 miles, from Malmö to Stockholm, also a most important line. The necessary power comes in part from the Central Block and in part from a private company.

The Riksdag voted in 1933 to electrify an additional 580 miles of state railroad, including the west coast line from Malmö to Gothenburg. This newest project was completed toward the end of 1936 and until 1945, when the state begins to develop new power resources, it will receive the greater part of the necessary current from private companies which have agreed to coöperate with the Royal Board of Waterfalls. With the completion of this last project, there are in all nearly 1,700 miles, about 40 per cent, of the railway lines of the state powered with electricity. Eighty per cent of the carriage on the state system, 50 per cent for all railway lines, public and private, is now done electrically. This requires an estimated 400,000,000 kilowatt hours a year, representing about 8 per cent of the total energy production of Sweden. For a country with abundant water power and virtually no coal reserves such a movement obviously strengthens the internal economy, both for peace- and wartime purposes.

The state railways occupy a position with relation to private railways that is to a certain degree analogous to the relationship between private and public power plants. The state rail system, skilfully and efficiently operated, serves to determine rates on the private lines. It is true, of course, that the private lines occupy a subsidiary position and are chiefly feeders for the main trunks owned by the state. In recent years the state has been trying to work out a rational transportation system for the whole country, coördinating rail, motor, water, and air, and assigning to each its proper place.

Motor bus competition has not been such a factor in Sweden as in the United States. Perhaps the principal reason for this is the schedule of railway fares, whereby the rate is increasingly lower for each mile that one travels. The first mile is so much, the second mile fractionally less, and so on. Because of this rate schedule motor busses are unable to compete effectively on long hauls.

Nevertheless they have been a factor. Then, too, as with the electric power system, the state has assumed the responsibility of sustaining rail service in remote and sparsely populated rural areas where the incentive of profit alone would not be sufficient to encourage operation. This was one of the reasons why, as the depression deepened, the state railways failed to earn their full interest charges. The annual interest charge at 5 per cent on the total capital is 15,276,000 kronor; in 1931 the state railways earned a surplus of 12,864,000 kronor or 2,412,000 less than the fixed charges. There was marked improvement in 1934.

Here are the figures for three years, showing revenues, operating expenses and surplus, all in kronor:

	1932	1933	1934
Passenger traffic	61,055,000	59,969,000	65,977,000
Freight traffic, except ore	77,510,000	79,199,000	90,945,000
Lapland ore	16,907,000	16,252,000	15,963,000
Other sources	10,673,000	10,721,000	10,914,000
TOTALS	166,145,000	166,141,000	183,799,000
Total operating costs, including payments to renewal fund in kronor	153,290,000	150,174,000	155,197,000
SURPLUS	12,855,000	15,967,000	28,602,000

The private railways suffered great losses from motor bus competition and the state was compelled to take over several failing lines. But even the private roads have begun to recover. A net loss of 2,000,000 kronor for 1933 was converted into a surplus of 7,000,000 kronor in 1934. Credit for a part of this extraordinary gain is given to a modernization program that has resulted in speeding up rail service. Some private lines paid dividends up to 5 per cent in 1934. Cities and smaller communities hold controlling blocks of stock in many of these private lines.

It should be said that the Scandinavians are ardent travelers. And since they are strongly conscious of their own past, their own traditions and background, they are given to exploring the Scandinavian peninsula. A large railway station, such as that at Stockholm, affords a curious study in the Scandinavian temperament during the holiday season. Each departing traveler must apparently endure the curious and solemn ritual of farewell that, one suspects, goes back at least to the time of the Vikings. The victim sits in his compartment with the singularly foolish expression that marks departing travelers the world over while outside a knot of his friends is gathered; he has thanked them for their gifts, they have said everything that can possibly be said and still they wait; then, just as the train is about to pull out they put their heads together and raise four lusty cheers, "Rah, rah, rah, rah!" Great bursts of cheering resound for each train that leaves the station.

In the beginning stages of air travel the state saw to it that rail and air lines were coördinated, preventing destructive competition between the two. Thus it was not until 1936 that there was an airline between Stockholm and Malmö although the Swedish Aërotransport Company has been in existence for nearly twelve years. Under the able direction of Capt. Carl Florman there has been a constant expansion, the latest line to open being that between Stockholm and Moscow.

At the outset the only line on which there was competition between rail and air was that between Malmö and Gothenburg. The air trip for this distance costs seventy-two kronor and the train trip forty kronor for first class, twenty for second, and fourteen for third. Inasmuch as the train takes six hours for the journey and the plane one hour and twenty minutes it would seem that the price was equitably adjusted between the two. Similarly, when air service was started between Stockholm and Malmö the traveler was made to pay a rather high premium for speed and there was reserved for those who are content to take a longer time at a lower price, travel by railroad.

During the summer there is overnight air mail service from Stockholm to the continent via Malmö so that letters mailed at the central post office in the capital before 6:30 P.M. are delivered in Berlin, London, or Paris the next morning. This summer service has been in effect several seasons and now work is under way on beacons and emergency landing fields which will make it possible to continue the mail line throughout the year.

The Swedish Aërotransport Company has had a most remarkable record for safety, not a single passenger being so much as scratched in the twelve years that the company has been in existence. Aërotransport planes flew 890,000 kilometers in 1934 and 1,250,000 kilometers in 1935. Up to March 31, 1935, 135,704 passengers had been carried. The main routes flown by Aërotransport are to a certain degree hazardous, particularly that between Stockholm and Helsingfors which is over the innumerable rocky, wooded islands of the Swedish and Finnish archipelagoes.

In May of 1935 the Riksdag voted to invest public funds in the Aërotransport Company, bringing it under the domination of the state. Prior to that time the line had received annual subsidies from the government. Coördination of air and rail traffic would be much simpler if both forms of transportation were under government ownership, it was decided. With the state owning the majority of the stock, most of the directors are now appointed by the government. The state director of air traffic undertook to revise, more or less experimentally, certain air rates during the season of 1935. In some instances it was found necessary to reduce the air rate in order to draw a larger amount of traffic. The Riksdag has approved the construction of several major airports, those for Eskilstuna and Örebro among others, and has shown great interest in plans for an air route to northernmost Sweden.

As the state owns the major means of transportation, so also it owns the major lines of communication, telephone and telegraph. The state telephone and telegraph system continued to return a sizeable surplus through the depression. The telephone system is one of the most efficient in the world, proof of that being the fact that there are more telephones in Stockholm, proportionately, than in any other European city—more than in many of the large cities of the United States. The cost of a full party line in Stockholm is about $20.50 a year to the householder. For this rate one may make an average of three outgoing calls a day and there is, of course, no restriction on the number of incoming calls.

What is most extraordinary to the foreign visitor is that one may make calls in French, English, and German as well as in Swedish through the assistance of special operators who serve during the tourist season. The dial system is being introduced in Stockholm and the larger cities. Long distance charges seem very modest. From Stockholm one may talk for three minutes to the most remote northern province for as little as thirty cents and it is not necessary to get up in the middle of the night to obtain this rate. For a call to Malmö, at the southern tip, the charge is about eighteen cents.

Here are operating figures for the telephone and telegraph system for two years, in kronor:

	1933	1934
Income	104,156,588	107,979,719
Operating expenses	64,260,268	63,877,821
Set aside for obsolescence	9,817,898	9,983,428
TOTAL OPERATING EXPENSES	74,078,166	73,861,249
NET SURPLUS	30,078,422	34,118,470
Percentage of capital invested, represented by surplus	8.67	9.60

The item of operating expense does not include interest on the capital invested in the public communication system. If one deducts from the net surplus, as shown above, interest on invested capital at the state rate, 4.66 per cent, the "dividend" to the state on operation of the telephone and telegraph system would still be a substantial one.

It is a long way from the airplane, the telephone, the radio, to the dark heart of the forests of Norrland and the skills of the foresters passed down from one generation to the next for untold centuries. And yet these two extremes come within the control of the government and they are related if only in that they have been made to serve the interests of the whole people.

VII

THE STATE AS MONOPOLIST

THE state monopolies that Sweden has created represent a more complex form of public control than the state ownership which has just been described. They represent more nearly a compromise between private and public ownership, a form that, in the argument of its proponents, unites the virtues of individual initiative and collective self-interest.

In the present phase of world transition this compromise form has attracted wide attention and it is probable that in the future even greater interest will center upon such experimental efforts to bridge the gap between old and new. Great Britain has undertaken in the British Broadcasting Corporation a major experiment in semiprivate, semipublic control over an important industry. Furthermore the British Labor party has indicated that it favors some such form for the early socialization of coal, the railroads, and other complex industries. What has been done in Sweden then with these public-private corporations has an especial significance, and particularly the steps that are contemplated for the future. It may well be that Sweden's most important contribution in economics and government lies here.

Liquor and tobacco were brought under a monopoly at about the same time. Corporations were created by law which were nominally private corporations. But the securities issued by these corporations represented only a slight fraction of their capitalization if they had been under outright private control. All the profits accruing to the two monopolies, beyond a limited dividend to those who hold the small amount of outstanding securities, go to the state. The state reserves the right to say who shall hold these securities. Certain of the directors on the boards of the two corporations are named by the state. As a matter of actual fact the state retains what is in effect the right to supervise the affairs of the two companies.

I asked the present managing director of the liquor monopoly, John Bergvall, why the state had set up this system of private operation under state supervision. Why had not the state itself gone into the liquor business and the tobacco manufacturing business? His answer was as follows:

In the liquor business it is essential to have very responsible employees. They must serve the public efficiently and courteously and they must be quite trustworthy. There must be a strong incentive to provide honest merchandise. We pay salaries that are somewhat above the level of state salaries. They are not as high as salaries in a wholly private corporation but they are higher than could be paid if we were a state enterprise. A middle salary, you understand, between public and private standards.

Likewise with the security of the job. Our workers have a sense of greater security than they would have in an ordinary company, but they do not have the same complete security that they would have if they were employed by the state under Civil Service. In this respect, too, it is a middle course. Then, also, in a business of this nature, it is highly desirable to be altogether free from recurrent political interference.

That is why we have worked out this middle form, between the ownership and operation of the state and the ownership and operation of private capital. It has worked very well for us and I believe that other nations might profitably study this form. It does not curb entirely the initiative of the individual, for in this system one may rise to a higher salary through superior efforts. The board would limit the salary eventually—one would never receive an excessive salary—but nevertheless the incentive for the individual is there.

This seemed such a logical answer that I have given it here in full. Various motives led to the creation of these two monopolies. With liquor, as is explained more fully in the following chapter, the state was motivated in large part by the desire for social control over the liquor trade, and it was finally realized that such control was impossible so long as there was a considerable element of private profit constantly impelling private business to increase the volume of trade.

In making tobacco a monopoly in 1915 the government was moved almost entirely by the need for additional revenue. Another reason was to keep the price of tobacco as low as possible in the face of the wartime blockades, but this was a secondary consideration. It was a conservative government that passed the law establishing an outright monopoly on the importation of unprocessed tobacco, the manufacture and wholesale distribution of cigars and cigarettes. The government had to find additional revenue to start the old-age pension system and the tobacco monopoly appeared the simplest solution.

The nature of the pension system should be explained here inasmuch as it is closely allied with the government monopolies. Everyone over the age of sixteen is required to contribute, in proportion to his income, to a compulsory old-age insurance system. The local communities are required to contribute to the central pension fund on behalf of those unable to make their own contributions. At the age of sixty-seven every citizen, regardless of his financial status, is entitled to a pension, the amount depending upon the size of his contributions to the system. This system is based upon actuarial principles and requires little or no outright support from the state.

For those whose cash income is not more than 100 kronor a year, the state has recently provided an enlarged supplementary income. For persons in rural areas this is 250 kronor; in medium-sized towns 350; and in Stockholm and Gothenburg 450. The state provides three fourths of this supplement and the commune the remainder. To encourage private companies to set up their own pension systems, the government, in determining whether an individual is entitled to supplementary income, counts as "privileged" a portion of the private pension. For example, a married man in Stockholm with a company pension of 600 kronor could count 400 kronor as "privileged"; this would leave 100 kronor each for himself and his wife and they would therefore be entitled to the supplement of 450 kronor each, plus approximately 140 kronor from their own contributions to the pension system. They would thus have a minimum pension of 1,640 kronor.

It was to pay for these state contributions to the pension program that the tobacco monopoly was originally set up. The government owns the common stock, with a nominal value of 31,088,000 kronor. There is outstanding only 1,072,000 in preferred stock, paying a dividend to the private individuals who hold it of 5 per cent. From 1915 to 1931 inclusive the state received in dividends from the tobacco monopoly 1,318,560,000 kronor which, even when spread over a period of sixteen years, is a considerable sum in the budget of any country.

What is equally important, the consumer can buy a good cigarette for the equivalent of about twenty-five cents for twenty, either Virginia or Turkish, and there are cheaper brands. When it is recalled that all tobacco must be imported, this price seems reasonable. The fact that there is a monopoly on the manufacture of raw tobacco does not prevent the importation of cigarettes from abroad, particularly from the United States. A high import duty is levied upon tobacco in manufactured form so that the ordinary American cigarette costs in Stockholm about fifty-five cents a package at par.

Many other European governments hold tobacco monopolies. Some governments have entered directly into the business of manufacturing tobacco products and all too often their cigarettes are not only bad but expensive. This may be proof that the Swedish practice is better in such a field—the form of a private company, dominated by the state, and operated primarily for its profit.

There is no doubt that this has given Sweden an advantage in world trade during the depression. For example, the wholesale liquor monopoly is now the largest single buyer of foreign wines, particularly French wines. In the course of the annual negotiations in Paris for wine shipments, the Swedes, by merely suggesting that German wines and Spanish wines are also of excellent quality, have been able virtually to dictate import quotas of Swedish lumber and newsprint to France. In the same way when buying tobacco Sweden has had a great deal to say about reciprocal purchases of Swedish products. This is superior, if only in that it is simpler, to the roundabout methods by which diplomacy negotiates so-called trade treaties. This direct barter is a form of world trade that is likely to become more and more common.

A combination private-public monopoly having been successful in the distribution of tobacco and liquor, it was available as a medium for the control of radio broadcasting. The significant social aspects of the radio were quickly perceived by the state, and the Telegraph Board was given entire authority over early experimental broadcasting. Many interests sought from the government the right to broadcast. Advertising agencies were keen to utilize this new potential source of profit. After mature deliberation the government recognized the claims of two groups, the newspapers of Sweden and the manufacturers of radio apparatus. These two groups were invited to form a limited dividend company in partnership with the government, along the lines of the already existing state monopolies.

This company, Radio Service, provides all radio programs. Radio listeners in Sweden never hear an advertisement. Only occasionally do they hear political discussion and then it is a round table with all factions represented. There is dissatisfaction, of course, with radio programs. Some listeners complain that the programs are too serious, too dull; others insist that they are too frivolous, too trivial. Radio audiences the world over seem to be notoriously disaffected. But the fact that the radio listener in Sweden is not constantly subjected to some form of persuasion, commercial or political, would seem to weigh heavily in favor of the Swedish system.

The Telegraph Board provides only the technical equipment for broadcasting. Revenue comes from an annual license fee of ten kronor, about $2.70, assessed against all radio sets. There are at present more than 650,000 licensed sets, which is one for about every other household. The gross revenue from licenses is more than $1,750,000. Of this, one third is apportioned to Radio Service to pay for the programs. This cost is about $500,000, including the limited dividend of 7 per cent paid to those who own the shares of the company—that is, the newspapers and the manufacturers of radio apparatus. Any unexpended balance out of this one third, after the programs have been paid for and the dividend has been declared, is returned to the state. In addition, of course, the government receives the other two thirds of the amount derived from license fees. The state's net profit from the radio monopoly is difficult to determine because the technical costs of broadcasting are included in the total costs of the Telegraph Board, which shows, at the end of each fiscal year, a blanket profit.

The need to find additional revenue with which to enlarge the old-age pension system brought the issue of state monopolies to the fore when the Social-Democrats came into power in 1932. The compulsory contributory phase of the system had worked well enough. The Central Pension Fund, into which all payments go, amounted at the end of 1933 to 675,000,000 kronor, so invested as to bring an average return of 4.65 per cent. The number of insured was 3,822,900 and since insurance does not begin until the age of sixteen this included virtually the entire population. Even the king's brother, Prince Eugen, upon reaching the age of sixty-seven, drew his first pension payment, 10 per cent annually of all the payments he had made to the fund.

The inadequacy of the pensions was, however, generally recognized. It was not only sound social policy but good politics for the Social-Democrats to propose marked increases in these pension rates. The maximum had been increased, for those who applied for the state pension after 1922, to 225 kronor to men and 215 kronor to women but even so they were woefully inadequate. The Social-Democrats declared that these payments should be increased so that no one would have to endure the stigma of poor relief or the poor house.

Conservatives answered that the old-age pension system had ceased to be an insurance system and that it was only a disguised form of charity. They pointed out that in 1933 there was contributed to pensions for the destitute aged 67,133,705 kronor, of which the central government paid 50,350,279 and municipalities and provinces the balance. This was in contrast to 7,242,499 distributed to those who had paid their premiums through the years. Denmark, the conservatives pointed out, had abandoned the entire insurance pretense and now gave straight pensions.

The Social-Democrats did not argue over mere terms. They talked in facts and figures. The Minister of Finance, Ernst Wigforss, in an address in Stockholm in 1935, estimated that the annual expenditure of the central government would jump from 57,000,000 kronor to 90,000,000 almost immediately under the proposed pension increases. By 1950 the cost, he estimated, would be 136,000,000 kronor a year. Where, he asked, would the additional 30,000,000 kronor for the budget of 1936–37 come from? It could be raised by increased taxes, but far more equitably, he argued, it could be obtained from new monopolies, in coffee and gasoline. Just so, he pointed out, the conservatives had paid for the original pension system twenty years before out of the revenue from the monopolies in liquor and tobacco.

Now, of course, neither coffee nor gasoline is produced in Sweden so that the needed revenue might have been raised easily enough by additional duties on these two commodities. But this would have the immediate effect of increasing the cost of coffee and gasoline to the consumer. And it happens that coffee is the favorite drink of the majority of the voters in the labor and Left Wing liberal parties and an increase in the duty which would scarcely affect the wealthy conservatives at all would strike an appreciable blow at the household budget of the mass of the people. Coffee corresponds in Sweden to the home distilling privilege of the farmers in France. It is a political symbol and a sacred one. The leaders of the left, it is scarcely necessary to add, treat this symbol with a profound respect.

"It is easy enough to increase the duty," the Minister of Finance said. "But who pays? The mass of persons with small incomes."

"On the other hand," he continued, "suppose that on a kilogram of coffee costing 3.50 kronor, there is a profit of 1 krona, and that we could save 25 per cent of that. That would give us ten million kronor in new state revenue. And suppose that we could save another 25 per cent in the cost of distribution. That would give us still another ten million."

What he meant, of course, was that the state by eliminating the element of profit, except for a safe margin of surplus, and by cutting out the cost of the middleman could thereby save 20,000,000 kronor which might be used to pay for higher pensions for the needy aged. This is the kind of realistic political argument that stirs the Swedes.

"But what about the liberty of individual initiative?" the conservatives demanded. "Yes," Wigforss answered, "you are all free now to become millionaires. How much do you want for that freedom? Would you not rather have a little more security?" And the campaign was on.

The possibility of international barter with monopolies in gasoline and coffee was an argument which the Social-Democrats used effectively. It might be possible, they pointed out, to make an advantageous trade with Russia whereby Soviet gasoline would be exchanged for Swedish machinery. Because refining is, of course, an outright state monopoly in Russia, the Soviets would be able to bargain in the course of such a deal within a very flexible price range. The government would have to take into account the political reaction to such a deal with the Soviets. There is a deep-seated fear of domination by Russia that goes back to the long struggle for supremacy in the Baltic. Mothers in the more remote rural provinces say to their children when they have been bad, "You are nothing but a little Russian," meaning a barbarian.

Strong opposition to these proposed new monopolies quickly developed. The conservatives brought out familiar arguments about the rights of the individual and the value of individual initiative. Mass meetings were held throughout the country and mass petitions were circulated which nearly a million persons signed, according to claims of the opposition. The proposed monopolies were an issue in the Stockholm municipal elections held in the spring of 1935 in which the Social-Democrats lost a few seats to the newly reorganized People's party, the strongest liberal group. But this might have been explained by the heavy gains which the Social-Democrats had made at the expense of the disunited liberals in previous contests.

At the height of the dispute Albin Johansson in a public statement announced his opposition to the new state monopolies. The conservatives welcomed him as an unexpected ally. But he was careful to make clear that his stand was in line with the view he has held for thirty years in opposition to monopoly price restrictions of any kind. The state has no more right to foster monopoly in the necessities of life than has private business, Johansson holds, emphasizing the danger of artificial price restrictions with resultant high price levels and the whole stream of evils that flows therefrom. Johansson's announcement weighed heavily against the proposed monopolies, it is conceded by the Social-Democrats.

The new pension increases will make poor relief unnecessary

for all but a small minority of the aged, the Social-Democrats
maintain. The amounts to be paid still seem slight to the outsider but the cost of living, particularly in the rural areas, remains fairly low. The wage level increased 80 per cent from
1913 to 1933, while the cost of living rose less than 50 per
cent. In 1926 the hourly rate had risen by 165 per cent, as compared to 1913, the daily wage by 123 per cent and the yearly
wage by 120 per cent. At the same time the pay of white collar
workers increased only 92 per cent over the 1913 level. This is
in direct contrast to the trend in the United States where the
manual worker has received an ever-decreasing share and the
white collar an ever larger proportion of the national income
since 1913. Consistently low prices have enhanced the workers'
purchasing power in Sweden.

To help pay for this newest extension of the social security
program a monopoly of the manufacture of munitions, under
state control and with most of the profits reserved for the state,
was also proposed. But here, as with the liquor monopoly, the
principal motive was not financial but social. A committee of
the Riksdag appointed to study this industry soon discovered
ramifications that linked it with world capitalism. The difficulty,
the impossibility for the present at least, of bringing the munitions business under state ownership illustrate the limitations
that Sweden faces in any program of social or economic change
which is more than superficial; it is after all a small country tied
into the complex network of interlocking capitalism.

The Riksdag committee found that the Krupp works of Germany, through a dummy corporation, owned about one third
of the shares of the Bofors Company, largest munitions manufacturer in Sweden, and that Flygindustri, an aviation manufacturing concern, was, in the words of Foreign Minister
Sandler, "nothing more than a branch of the German Junkers
concern." What had happened was that when the Treaty of
Versailles forbade the manufacture of arms in Germany, the
Bofors Company acquired certain patent rights and designs
from Krupp in order to be able to fill repeat orders from
Krupp's foreign customers; in payment Bofors issued shares to
a Swedish holding company, A.B. Boforsintressenter, organized

February 12, 1921, with a nonentity as sole director. The charge was made, emanating, it is said, from the Schneider-Creusot munitions interests by way of the French press, that many arms shipments from Bofors, marked for a South American destination, never left Hamburg, the port presumably of transshipment. This the Bofors management indignantly denied and investigation by a Riksdag committee failed to substantiate the charge.

The Swedish public was profoundly shocked by these disclosures even though the Bofors management insisted there had been no German interference in the direction of the company. In the debate that followed in the Riksdag all Leftward and moderate parties agreed that government control of the munitions industry was necessary; the conservative Right thought that Sweden should not be the first to take such a stand. Leaders of the Right were of the opinion that a law eliminating foreign holding companies, which became effective July 1, 1935, was sufficient to put an end to foreign influence over Bofors. The Communists were for an outright government monopoly in munitions.

Prime Minister Per Albin Hansson in the course of the debate in the Second Chamber confronted his colleagues with the practical difficulties of bringing about such a monopoly. The situation was serious enough, he said, particularly in view of the attempt of another foreign power, later identified as France, to gain a foothold at Bofors through the powerful Schneider-Creusot group. The Bofors management professed to be willing enough to coöperate in eliminating foreign ownership but the dummy who held the stock was not willing nor was Germany in the least interested in surrendering its strategic position.

What came out of this difficult situation was a compromise. It is such a compromise as absolutists would scorn but it is in the tradition of the functional compromises by means of which Sweden has made a slow kind of progress during the past twenty to thirty years. All new munitions plants, and after January 1, 1938, all existing munitions plants, must have a special license from the government to operate. This has been interpreted as giving the state the power of life and death over the munitions business. One of the effective arguments raised by the

Social-Democrats on behalf of this compromise was that it accorded with Sweden's formal approval of the American proposal at Geneva for licensing munitions plants.

Under the old law Swedish munitions plants were required to obtain only a special government license for exports. They must have a permit to operate under the new law and must allow a government inspector access to their books at all times, so that all orders on hand will be known to the government. The government also has the right to decide what constitutes materials of war and to revoke licenses at any time. Furthermore, under the new law all agents of foreign munitions plants must obtain permits before they can do business in Sweden.

It is interesting to note the pragmatic reason that the Riksdag investigating committee gave for rejecting the Communist demand for an outright monopoly of munitions manufacture. Under government ownership, said the committee, no export orders could be filled and without exports the efficiency of domestic munition plants could not be sustained. The management of Bofors pointed out that it was thanks to expert technical advice from Krupp's that Bofors had been able to maintain its high standards and compete on the world market.

To comply with the new law against holding companies the German shares were sold to a syndicate headed by Axel Wenner-Gren. Wenner-Gren is the newest Swedish Crœsus, his rapidly mounting fortune built upon a world-wide trade in patented household devices. He succeeded in building up an extraordinary world-wide sales organization. And on the bargain counter he bought up the Kreuger pulp and cellulose properties for one tenth of their cost.

Munitions have not played an important part in Sweden's export trade. From 1927 to 1931 war materials were valued at about one per cent of all Swedish exports. They represented only seven tenths of a per cent of Sweden's total industrial production during that time. Since 1931, the average value of war goods exported has increased from 13,200,000 kronor to 20,-300,000 kronor.

But although the munitions business represents only a minute fraction of Sweden's economic life, it illustrates the difficulties that confront a small country dependent upon world trade and world finance. Swedish capitalism has close ties with German capitalism. A decision to nationalize the munitions industry would have meant an intensive struggle which apparently the Social-Democrats were unwilling to face. It may be true, as their critics on the left so often charge, that they think too entirely in terms of dependence upon world trade. But obviously, the Social-Democrats reply, in Sweden one cannot think in terms of a continent and continental self-sufficiency.

At a recent session of the Riksdag there was prolonged discussion of the broadcasting monopoly. One faction was for giving the state outright control of the semiprivate company that now has a monopoly from the government. In the end the two chambers agreed to a compromise whereby the present arrangement will be continued, but with additional government representation in the management of the company.

The extension of the monopoly system is likely to be a major issue in the future. How far the Social-Democrats are willing to push this issue is a question. A large and vociferous opposition has developed. But it is an issue which the Social-Democrats cannot ignore if they are to expand the program of social security which at present can hardly be considered liberal, even with the recent increases granted by the Riksdag. To finance this kind of expansion the state must levy funds in such a way that the very classes to be benefited by the social security program must not be made to pay for those benefits by a tax which would certainly lower their standard of living. It is plain that the cost of these benefits, if they are to be of any real aid, must come from the wealth of the owning class. Both the liquor and the tobacco monopoly have demonstrated that that wealth is more directly reached through diversion of profit to the state than through the indirect method of a heavy tax upon those profits.

VIII

LIQUOR CONTROL THAT WORKS

THE efforts of the Nordic peoples to prohibit the use of alcohol make a singularly fascinating chapter in the history of reform. This impulse toward prohibition would seem to come out of a curious dichotomy, a deeply buried conflict between the secret forces of good and evil inherent in the Nordic temperament. An unhappy irresolution has all too often resulted from this conflict, and the unfortunate Nordic has gone from one violent extreme to the other.

Sweden was very close to prohibition in 1909. In that year the government issued an emergency decree, forbidding the manufacture and sale of intoxicants during the general strike, a period of almost six weeks. This seemed to have such a salutary effect on the entire population that ardent prohibitionists decided it was time to push their cause to what seemed certain victory. They forgot, or they chose to ignore, the fact that it was an emergency measure and therefore no real test of prohibition. Their zeal prevailed and a voluntary plebiscite was conducted which showed 1,884,298 votes for prohibition and only 16,718 votes against.

This was in the nature of a consultative plebiscite and while it was not binding, the prohibitionists immediately set up a clamor for a bone-dry law. The moderate faction argued that although the vote for prohibition was large, it represented only about 51 per cent of the total voting strength of the nation. They insisted that the issue was far too important to be determined by such a narrow majority; that a law affecting so profoundly the habits of the entire people should have the sanction of at least two thirds of the voters.

It was at this point in the prohibition battle that a young Stockholm physician, Dr. Ivan Bratt, emerged as the leader of the moderates. Dr. Bratt had made a careful study of the problem of alcohol in a complex society and on the basis of that study he had concluded not only that the enforcement of prohibition was impossible but that the attempt to enforce it would work disastrous consequences on the general law of the land and on the public attitude toward the law.

Often in a democracy the voice of moderation is a still, small voice crying in the wilderness, but in this instance Dr. Bratt had the support of a very influential section of society. Friends at court and in the government did all they could to aid him in putting across his ideas. He began by writing a series of forceful articles which were published in the Stockholm *Dagens Nyheter*. Eloquently Dr. Bratt argued that no act could be condemned as a crime which many reputable citizens regarded as an ancient and inalienable right. This sounds rather like the debate over prohibition repeal in the United States. The fact is that Sweden debated first and acted afterwards.

Largely as a result of Dr. Bratt's propaganda for moderation the Riksdag, disposed to move cautiously in any circumstances, appointed a committee of eleven to study the liquor question and submit a report. This committee was made up of ten prohibitionists and Dr. Bratt. Swedish prohibitionists are not unlike the American variety and yet Dr. Bratt, a minority of one, was able to bring the other ten members of the committee around to his point of view. No more remarkable tribute to his powers of persuasion could be imagined.

Dr. Bratt had worked out by this time a fairly definite scheme for liquor control. It was based upon the Gothenburg system, then in force throughout most of Sweden. The Swedes have been a hard-drinking people. Eighty years ago they consumed ten gallons of intoxicants per capita each year. And when it is realized that this includes the entire population, down to infants in arms, the capacity of those of drinking age is seen to have been on the scale of the Vikings themselves. In 1865, with the adoption of the Gothenburg system, an effort was made to check this flow of spirits. The new system achieved certain reforms. The old-fashioned saloon was abolished and the sale of spirits by the glass was transferred to restaurants. The manufacture of the national drink, brännvin, potato brandy, was restricted to certain private companies with dividends limited by

law, the balance accruing to the state. For the sale of brännvin
to be consumed off the premises 120 local limited-dividend companies were formed.

Prohibitionists were fond of saying that under the Gothenburg plan the saloon had been transferred to the home. And
they had significant statistics to support their arguments. The
death rate from chronic alcoholism was high, averaging 2.18
per 100,000 for 1911. While per-capita consumption had
dropped to less than two gallons, for the decade from 1900 to
1910, drunkenness was common and it was reflected in crimes
of violence. In the city of Stockholm, for example, there were
17.86 such crimes per 10,000 as against 6.89 for all Sweden.

But Dr. Bratt saw that the Gothenburg plan had made a beginning at what, in his opinion, is essential to any form of liquor control—"disinterested management." That is a management with no interest in the profits and therefore no interest in
pushing sales. Once in answer to Americans who came to him
for help out of their dilemma of prohibition, Dr. Bratt put it
very well: "The fight against human excesses . . . is difficult.
The fight against profiteering purveyors of alcohol is difficult.
The fight against these two powers combined is hopeless."

The Stockholm System Company, operating under the old
Gothenburg plan, had to apply early in 1914 for a new charter.
Dr. Bratt organized a rival company and applied to the Town
Council of Stockholm for the charter, granted under the law, of
course, to only one operating company. With the aid of some of
the prohibitionists on the council whom he had won over, Dr.
Bratt got the grant. And at once he proceeded to put his own
system into effect. It was a test, and a bold test, of the principles
he had advocated.

Control under Dr. Bratt's system was to be exerted upon the
individual. The people of Stockholm were told in February of
1914 that no one would be allowed to buy any form of liquor
until he or she had obtained a *motbok*—a pass book—from the
Stockholm System. The citizen applying for a motbok was required to state his age, occupation, capital, income, size of family, and record and reputation for sobriety, very much as though
he were applying for a life insurance policy or a license to drive
an automobile. The analogy with the latter is very close. There

is the same implication: that the use of liquor, like the use of an automobile, involves a certain degree of social control and social responsibility which the user must possess if he is to be given a license by the state.

The other phase of Dr. Bratt's plan involved the concentration of all manufacture, sale and importation of alcoholic beverages in a limited-dividend monopoly. Soon after the introduction of his system Dr. Bratt began buying up the private companies engaged in the liquor trade. He offered them a reasonable price and if they were unwilling to sell, he made it quite clear that he possessed the power to destroy them by merely refusing to buy their wares. It was not long before this remarkable man had brought the liquor business, figuratively speaking, under a single firm name, with private profit eliminated except for a modest dividend upon a small share capital held under strict supervision. Supported by the state, the Bratt system spread throughout Sweden until finally it was made obligatory under a law that became effective January 1, 1919.

As organized today, the wholesale liquor trade of Sweden is carried on by the Wine and Spirits Central, with a relatively small capital, about $4,000,000. Of this, $108,000 is in ordinary shares, returning $5\frac{1}{2}$ per cent, owned by a syndicate of ten persons approved by the government. The ordinary shares are the only voting shares; they may not be sold without permission of the government and then only to a person approved by the government. The balance of the capital, $3,942,000, is in preferred nonvoting shares, which pay a maximum dividend of 5 per cent. Of the board of eight directors of this company, four, including the chairman, are named by the government, and four by the holders of the voting shares.

The retailing of spirits and wine is in the hands of what are called System companies, 122 in number for the whole country. These are organized on the same plan as the wholesale company. The shareholders of the System companies receive only a 5 per cent dividend and the total capital is so small that the amount paid in dividends by all of them is only about $25,000. Of the board of directors made up of five members, the chairman is named by the Royal Board of Control, appointed by the government, which has supreme authority over liquor sales in

Sweden; two are named by the local authorities in the community in which the individual company operates; and two are chosen by the shareholders.

In the fifteen years that he directed the Swedish liquor system Dr. Bratt made many minor changes in this plan but the two basic principles—disinterested management through the elimination of profits and control of the individual by passbook, or license—were the real reasons, in Dr. Bratt's opinion, for its success. At the outset Dr. Bratt allowed all holders of motboks a maximum quota of spirits, about four and one quarter American quarts, a month. He discovered that the majority did not require more than half of this amount and that the excess was leading to trading, bootlegging, and other abuses of the system. Before long Dr. Bratt had classified all liquor purchasers and had issued their motboks accordingly.

An unmarried man can obtain no passbook at all until he is twenty-five years old and even after that his allowance is low. The maximum of four and a quarter quarts is granted only to a special class of individuals who have demonstrated that they are qualified to use this quantity. A single woman who earns her living is entitled to a passbook, if she is not too young, but her allowance is low, varying from one or two quarts a year to one or two quarts every three months. A married woman can obtain a passbook but not if her husband already owns one. And, of course, chronic alcoholics and habitual drunkards, criminals, and others who are socially irresponsible are forbidden to own a motbok.

But Dr. Bratt was not too arbitrary in laying down the administrative framework of his system. If, for example, you are having a large family festival or entertaining out of town guests, you merely go to your System store, state the facts briefly, and you are allowed to buy an extra amount of spirits. There has never been any restriction on the sale of light wines and only mild restriction on the heavier wines such as port and Madeira. Domestic beer that contains less than 3.2 per cent of alcohol by weight is sold without hindrance in licensed stores in "wet" localities. It must be remembered that local option prevails throughout the country and that more than 2,200 of Sweden's 2,400 districts are dry, although intoxicants may be taken into a dry district for individual consumption. Dr. Bratt was from the first determined to make his system fit rational human needs and to avoid any attempt to force human beings to fit into an arbitrary system.

Prices have never been high. Dr. Bratt believed that exorbitant prices force a kind of prohibition upon the lower income groups and inevitably give rise to the just charge of class discrimination. In normal times and under normal currency exchange, Scotch whiskey costs from $2.28 to $4.15 a short quart, 26 ounces. Burke's Irish Whiskey is $2.29 a quart and Hiram Walker's Bourbon $2.75. More important to the mass of consumers is the cost of brännvin, which ranges from sixty-six cents to ninety-two cents a liter. The cheapest of Bordeaux wines is forty-seven cents a bottle, sauternes from ninety cents to a dollar, champagnes from $2.25 for 1921 Veuve Cliquot to $4 for Mumm's Cordon Rouge, 1921. These prices compare favorably with prices on the continent, particularly when it is considered that import costs must be added, except for brännvin.

Many people found fault with the Bratt system. The newspapers quarreled over it angrily even though it was shown that it had had a relatively slight effect on their advertising revenue inasmuch as competitive brands were still at liberty to proclaim their virtues in the press. Statistics very soon began to show that the system was working. It had served to reduce substantially the amount of alcohol consumed and that was what really interested Dr. Bratt. In the first five years in which the system was in operation there was a 42 per cent decrease in the consumption of wines and liquors and in the next two years it dropped approximately another 10 per cent. And there were innumerable figures, on drunkenness, the incidence of crime, alcoholic insanity, to buttress the plain and simple fact that the Swedes were drinking less than they ever had before in their history.

From time to time Dr. Bratt found that adjustments were necessary. Thus the restrictions in Stockholm on sales by the bottle were quickly reflected in increased sales by the glass in licensed restaurants. In order to check this Dr. Bratt ruled that a restaurant customer had to buy cooked food of a certain value in order to get liquor. Before three o'clock in the afternoon the restaurant patron was limited to seven and a half centiliters and after that hour to fifteen centiliters. Roughly, fifteen centiliters is three fourths of the capacity of an ordinary water glass.

In his effort to achieve "disinterested management" Dr. Bratt had not overlooked the restaurants. The System companies have the sole right to license private restaurants to sell liquor. Most higher priced restaurants in the cities and towns are privately owned, under license. But even in these private cafés the profit element in the sale of liquor has been greatly restricted.

The Wine and Spirits Central, through its control of the wholesale prices, fixes the amount of spirits which each private restaurant may sell at a profit. For example, in the Opera House in Stockholm are several restaurants, among them the finest in the city, under private license to the same firm that operates the Grand Hotel. The restaurants in the Opera House are allowed to sell 20,000 liters of spirits a year at a profit. On spirits sold above this amount the restaurant makes no profit; the management loses money in fact on the handling of all liquor above the assigned quota. Obviously there is no incentive to induce patrons to drink more than they might normally do. In addition, the largest System companies, the one in Stockholm and the one in Gothenburg, maintain a chain of excellent moderate-priced restaurants at which spirits and wines are sold.

Although each new crop of statistics demonstrated that the system was working, its originator found himself nevertheless constantly under fire from opposing camps, the prohibitionists on the one side and the passionate advocates of personal liberty on the other. The latter group found the device of the motbok an outrageous invasion of their privacy. And this has been the comment of some American observers of the Bratt system. Americans, they have insisted, would never submit to this form of individual control.

But there seems little justification for this. Actually the examination, as it has been modified in recent years, is not as inclusive as an insurance examination, not even as comprehensive as the examination for a driver's license in a state such as Massachusetts. A young man applying for a passbook today must fill out a formal application blank in which he gives his full name, date and place of birth, occupation and place of employment, telephone number, residence and postoffice address, the parish in which he is registered and how long he has been registered there, and his last previous place of registration. He must state whether he is married, maintains a household, together with the names, ages and birthdays of all persons more than twenty-one years of age in his household, and whether he has ever held a passbook before. If he rents a room in a house in which others are living, he must give their names and ages, and he must state the amount of taxes he has paid and whether he is in arrears for the last three years. On the last line he must estimate the amount of spirits which he will want to purchase each month.

This seems reasonable, particularly when it is remembered that this information is put in a private file open only to officials of the System companies and the police. A young man of good repute would receive his passbook with little formality and within a short waiting period. He would be told his quota and the number of the retail store to which he was assigned and thenceforward he would buy his liquor very much after the fashion of private citizens all over the world, subject always to the two liter, or three liter, or four liter—the last if he has a household of his own—limit on quantity.

If his drinking habits are orthodox, as are those of a large majority of the System patrons, then he may never hear from the liquor officialdom again. But these officials will have a fairly good idea, nevertheless, of how the young man drinks. If, for example, he buys his full allowance of spirits in the two or three days immediately after the first of the month and thereafter buys a quantity of heavy wine, he is sure to come under the surveillance of the company. His record of purchases is carefully studied in any circumstance. He may be called in to explain and his allowance of spirits may be reduced, or his liquor purchases may be budgeted, to a half liter a week or a liter every two weeks.

There are sterner measures that may be applied if the young man repeats his offense or is several times arrested for drunkenness. The privilege that goes with his passbook may be temporarily suspended. And finally his motbok may be revoked.

This is not a punishment, not a disciplinary measure. It is a method of social control applied to an individual who has demonstrated his unfitness to have a certain special privilege. And while it is a powerful weapon, Professor Walter Thompson, whose comprehensive study of the Swedish liquor system, *The Control of Liquor in Sweden,* was published in 1935, finds that the System employs this weapon "justly, mercifully, and with an eye to individual and social consequences." It is always a measure of last resort, reluctantly used, for the directors of the System are well aware that it may send the individual to illicit sources to satisfy his thirst.

Of the 62,519 passbooks revoked in 1930, less than one tenth, 5,975, were revoked for misuse of intoxicants, according to Professor Thompson's analysis of the statistics for that year. This was out of a total of 1,222,969 passbooks outstanding in 1930, 1,096,906 issued to men and 126,063 to women. More than half of the motboks were revoked because the holders had died or changed their residence. A total of 8,765 were revoked because the holder was receiving charity or was in arrears in taxes. Even the figure 5,975 is high, according to Professor Thompson, because it includes those excluded because they had engaged in the bootleg liquor trade or had done compulsory labor.

But, of course, as Professor Thompson points out, this is not an index to the misuse of intoxicants in Sweden. Every other method is employed to check "overindulgence" before recourse is had to this final step. And furthermore there is the startling fact that passbook holders represented less than a fifth of those arrested for drunkenness in 1930. The flow of bootleg liquor has by no means been stopped although there are good reasons to believe that it is gradually being diminished.

Liquor was a considerable source of revenue to the state even under the Gothenburg system. Under the Bratt system it has yielded an enormous return year after year. In 1931, for example, when the depression had begun to cause a marked decline in consumption, the national liquor bill, at the System companies, was approximately $48,240,000. Of this amount the state received $28,408,000, or 58.7 per cent of the whole, in taxes and in profits of the Wine and Spirits Central and the System companies. And this does not include taxes paid to local government units. Nor does it include the considerable revenue from the malt tax levied on the brewers.

In 1932 the excise taxes were increased but even before this it is estimated that the income from the liquor trade amounted to about one sixth of the state's entire revenue. All estimates are too moderate, according to Professor Thompson, because they do not include numerous indirect taxes paid by brewers, restaurateurs, and persons employed in the liquor business. It is not improbable, in Professor Thompson's opinion, that the Swedish government realizes in normal times $50,000,000 a year from liquor. It is scarcely necessary to point out the importance of such a source of revenue in a country the size of Sweden.

Laws providing what shall be done with the revenue from liquor were passed with a view to removing the temptation of the state itself, or any unit of the state, seeking to encourage the consumption of liquor as a source of revenue. The revenue from liquor may not be used for general budgetary purposes, nor is the government allowed to use it in computing the budget. As prescribed by law, it is used in three ways: to promote temperance in a variety of ways, including the support of homes for the corrective treatment of alcoholics and habitual drunkards; for compensating the cities and rural communes, the counties and the agricultural associations, for relinquishing their claims upon this revenue; and for the amortization of the national debt. The government, according to Professor Thompson, has not been above the expedient of borrowing from this fund which, in 1931, approximated about $25,000,000.

Dr. Bratt decided in 1928 to retire. He had given nearly twenty years to establishing the method of liquor control that bears his name. His children were of college age and he would need a larger income to pay for their education than he could get in the service of the liquor monopoly, even in the capacity of director of the Stockholm System Company. For he had held consistently to the policy of salaries on a level between those paid by the state and those paid by private business, that is, not low and not high. Private industry was only too eager to bid for Dr. Bratt's services and he went to Paris shortly after his retirement as representative of S.K.F., the Swedish ball-bearing firm. With him he could take the satisfaction of a job well done and the praise of even those who had been at the outset his bitterest opponents. In the twenty years of his service he had learned a great deal about the habits of human beings in relation to the use of alcohol, which is equivalent, perhaps, to wisdom about human beings in general. In a kind of valedictory not long before his retirement Dr. Bratt said some very trenchant things about the use of alcohol in relation to society which seem to me so sane that I have quoted them in part here:

In my mind, if there is any index which is utterly valueless, it is the figure for per capita consumption. In fact, I believe, and have always gone on the assumption, that in each country only a portion of the use of liquor is to be considered injurious or anti-social.

We have seen how Denmark has reduced her consumption through the simple means of imposing a high tax on spirits. It is probably fair to say that the consumption of all individuals, speaking in a broad way, was reduced equally, and that the curtailment is reflected in the noninjurious consumption as well as in that which is injurious. The result accomplished, while it may be salutary, does not seem to me the one which should be sought.

Let me assume for the purpose of discussion that of the total alcoholic consumption of a nation, 70 per cent is not injurious and 30 per cent is. It seems clear to me that our problem is to attack the 30 per cent and not disturb the people who comprise the 70 per cent. I believe that in Sweden we have come as close to the desired result as is possible, or I believe that it is fair to say that we have eliminated three quarters of the injurious consumption without disturbing more than possibly one fifth of the harmless drinking that was taking place before the system was put into effect.

I believe that the question of reducing injurious consumption and leaving the rest alone is dependent mainly upon a proper system of control.

This, then, is the system and the man who created it. It was built upon and adapted to the habits of a people for whom drinking and eating—conviviality—are of the first importance. It has been suggested that this may have been because the terms on which man has lived in this northern land have not been easy. But whatever the reason, even the most casual visitor is made aware of the high value that the Swede puts upon food and drink—upon good food and drink.

There is first of all the factor of the climate. The winters are long and dark and pervaded with a penetrating damp chill. The human body can take large quantities of food and with it large quantities of drink. The Swede can dispel the gloom of winter with the distilled warmth of brännvin. A fifth of the country is beyond the Arctic Circle, the greater part of it is on a parallel with Yukon, Alaska. Strong drink is a refuge from the bitter weather.

But it is more than that—more than a mere physical need. The drinking habits of this people are woven into the cere-monial pattern of their lives. They are regulated by an ancient formalism, a deeply rooted tradition that has survived the inter-nationalism of the past two decades. I recall a small luncheon party at the home of Count and Countess Sparre in Stockholm. The Americans had been wined and dined in ceremonious fash-ion as members of a semiofficial delegation to the Swedish hous-ing exposition of 1930. The Sparres' young daughter-in-law had said to us that now we would escape from formality and from speeches. But we were hardly seated when our host rose and with a warm graciousness announced that in his land it was the custom to make a speech of welcome to one's guests and he would now do so.

When even a small group are dining together, something of a ritual is observed. At each place there is a glass of brännvin, a little larger than a liqueur glass. This is not to be taken up and sipped casually. At a signal from the host all the guests take up their glasses, bow to him and to each other, repeat the saluta-tion, "Skål!" and then, and then only, drain the glass. This may sound solemn and a little pompous but in actuality it is not. A brief ceremony, it serves to unite the company in a pleasant bond.

Ancient custom requires that the host and the hostess "skål" separately each guest at the table. This is done with wine, fortu-nately for sobriety. The host, and in her turn the hostess, looks down the table at the honored guest, catches his eye, raises his glass and repeats, "Skål." So he goes around the table. The hostess has in recent years been excused from this duty and even the host in traveled families has neglected it. Elaborate rules governing the skåling of guests of various rank have become the subject for jesting reference rather than serious observance among the younger generation. Thus in skåling an officer one was formerly required to hold one's glass even with a certain button on the officer's tunic, the level depending on his rank. What is remarkable is not that certain of the more complex of these traditions have been allowed to lapse but that they have survived so hardily in a world given more and more to a careful uniformity.

To the visitor from abroad the first fiery draught of brännvin is a test of self-composure. The uninitiated weep involuntarily, they are speechless. But it is preceded and followed by the manifold hors d'oeuvre comprising the genuine *smörgåsbord*. According to custom one must first eat a little of the smörgåsbord, drink one's glass of brännvin, and perhaps an additional half glass, and then finish up the smörgåsbord. The latter runs an .extraordinary gamut, from fish through hot dishes and several kinds of salad, to various cheeses. And it is followed by from three to five regular courses. The head of even the simplest household takes a pride in the number of dishes that are set out in the smörgåsbord. These may include on a special occasion in a working-class household a half dozen different kinds of fish, prawns, jellied eel, delicious salmon prepared in two or three ways, pickled herring and herring salad; four or five hot dishes and two or three salads with several cheeses; and with all this *knäckebröd* and sweet butter.

If the Swedes are given to generous hospitality in their homes, they are also great diners-out as the number and quality of the restaurants in cities and towns throughout the land prove. It is instructive to see groups at dinner on the Opera terrace or on the delightful roof garden at Hasselbacken, on a chilly night in June, swathed in rugs, determined that, the season to eat out of doors having arrived, they will observe the proper custom.

College students celebrating the end of the term in the late spring traditionally eat themselves "fast." The host has taken a dozen of his friends of both sexes to dinner at the Gyldene Freden. They have had brännvin with several kinds of wine, they have had Swedish punch or cognac at the end of the din-ner, and then they have lingered through the evening, with whiskey and soda, perhaps. The check comes and the host finds he hasn't enough money to pay it. Perhaps among them all they are unable to raise the price of the bill. They have eaten them-selves "fast" and they must appeal by telephone to a friend to come and bail them out. In their love of hospitality, of food and drink, the Swedes are given, prohibitionists and reformers often complain, to a kind of improvidence and competitive spending that is not unlike the similar phenomenon of keeping-up-with-the-Joneses in America.

This is enough to make clear that Swedish drinking customs have not been essentially changed by the Bratt system. Drinking has been curtailed, reduced, limited. But the personal liberty school has had little opportunity to use that sinister word, "regimentation." What is perhaps most significant is that legis-lation followed a period of experimentation. The system was tested before it was made the law of the land.

What Professor Thompson stresses in his study, and he is as objective in his analysis as one could possibly ask, is the feeling among most groups of the essential fairness of the Bratt system. It is not class legislation. The organized temperance crowd does not approve and has insisted from the beginning on the superi-ority of the Danish system of control by very high prices. But of this Professor Thompson says:

High prices in Denmark have placed spirits out of the reach of a large group of diligent and responsible people with limited purchasing power. This largely explains the tremendous reduction in per-capita consumption. But, compared with Sweden, temperance has not kept pace with this reduction. A study made by Miss Schultz leads one to wonder if the beneficial effects revealed by Danish statistics have not been greatly exaggerated. Comparing Copenhagen with Stockholm, Gothenburg, and Malmö, she finds that the three Swedish cities, since 1913, have shown a greater improvement than the Danish metropolis with regard to drunkenness in general and drunkenness among women and young people. To this the Dane might facetiously reply, "Natu-rally, Stockholm is in greater need of improvement than Copenhagen." That is true. In 1931, there was still a far greater number of drunks reported per capita in Stockholm than in Copenhagen. But, after allowing for the ups and downs, comparative figures show that while drunkenness decreased in the Swedish cities during the decade from 1921 to 1931, it increased in Copenhagen.

The temperance factions complain, too, that the system of individual control has not ended the bootleg trade. As Professor Thompson points out, however, the only way to end bootlegging is to abolish all restrictions and reduce the price of liquor as low as possible. Sweden's combined coastline is approximately the coastline of the United States from Maine to Florida. It is highly irregular and strewn with numerous small islands. To complicate the problem, Sweden's neighbors to the north, Finland and Norway, both have had a try at prohibition which attracted numerous rumrunners from the southern shores of the Baltic. But despite these handicaps the best information is that the amount of smuggled liquor is very small as compared to the amount of legal liquor sold and consumed.

Proof that the system works is contained in the report of the commission appointed by the Riksdag in 1928 to investigate, and, if necessary, to revise the method of liquor control. No one wholly approves of the system, this report shows, but there has been no substitute for it on which all could agree. Certain changes in the organization of the System companies have been suggested. A new agency is proposed to promote temperance. The commission recommends that certain minor and annoying restrictions be revoked.

But basically the system survived the intense scrutiny of the commission. The profit incentive has been eliminated. The opportunities for graft and the evils of bureaucracy are reduced to a minimum by the form of the monopoly, half private and half public. Every index points to the fact that harmful drinking, to use Dr. Bratt's expression, has been greatly reduced. It has been adjusted to the needs and habits of a people rooted in tradition and ancient habit. It has, in short, met the pragmatic test that Sweden applies to social reforms. And it illustrates the Swedish skill at effective compromise; between the right of the individual and the imperative demands of a complex society; between extreme dry and extreme wet; between those who would exploit every human need and desire for the sake of profit and those who would compel human beings to fit into an arbitrary pattern.

IX

SOCIALISTS, KING, AND CAPITALISTS

GUSTAF V has been a good king to his people. He is modest, thrifty, decent, kindly, all qualities which the Swedes admire. For nearly thirty years he has served as a simple and resolute symbol of the state, its integrity, its dignity, its strength. And by virtue of a genial sense of humor he has remained at the same time a very human and appealing figure, without the forbidding solemnity that ordinarily attaches to state symbols.

This symbol of the king is one of the things the Swedes have preserved out of the past; not as a museum piece, an antiquity, but as a part of the life of the nation, lending color and warmth to the everyday business of government. Like the king, the king's palace in Stockholm is characteristic of the land and the people. Its simple mass rises, a square, mauve-colored rock, from one of the principal islands on which the city is built. Small white steamers come and go in the broad expanse of water before the palace and the fishermen are busy all day long and far into the dusk with their big round nets, almost under the king's windows.

It is an appropriate home for the hard working ruler of a democracy which is governed from the Left. King Gustaf and the members of his family have always been conscientious about their jobs. As though aware of the stern demands of an age that has not been especially tolerant of kings, they have been more than decorative. The king himself has been pretty much occupied with the rôle of ruler; it is a full time assignment. But the crown prince, Gustaf Adolf, is a professional archæologist of note who has made important contributions to the museums of Sweden. Prince Eugen, one of the king's brothers, is a painter of merit who did one of the big mural decorations in the Town Hall. Prince Carl, another brother, is head of the Swedish Red Cross and not the nominal head either but a working executive who goes to his office each working day. And the others manage to occupy their time usefully, in the army, in the navy, or in some branch of the government.

This is true, of course, of all Scandinavian royalty. Those dissolute houses that are now in exile might well have looked to the north for instruction in the art of being royal in a modern democracy. In Copenhagen the Danish royal family preserves the same simplicity and the same earnest concern over the welfare of the country that one finds among Sweden's royalty. One of the Danish princesses is a photographer's retoucher. Norwegian royalty for the most part lives a rugged outdoor existence, immensely interested in carrying out certain experiments with dairy cattle and modern dairy practice. All this is in striking contrast to the behavior of a good many other European monarchies in recent decades.

It is hardly more than a century ago that the first Bernadotte was invited to Sweden to become heir to the throne succeeding a childless king, the last of a line that flourished through the sixteenth, seventeenth, and eighteenth centuries. The Bernadottes were of good petit bourgeois stock, from the little mountain district of Béarn in the Pyrenees. Jean Baptiste Bernadotte, a valiant and distinguished soldier, became one of Napoleon's marshals. His invitation to Sweden in 1810 saved him from the catastrophe that overtook Napoleon and his principal aides. The first Bernadotte to rule in Sweden became King Karl Johan XIV.

Karl Johan's descendants continue to rule, producing sturdy sons and daughters. At the same time the Bernadotte line has been carried on in France, often on humble levels. The present crown prince had this brought home to him while on a yachting cruise in the Mediterranean some years ago. The party put into a small fishing port to have some work done on the boat. The crown prince struck up a conversation with the man who directed the repairs. It developed that his name was Bernadotte and inquiry as to his native home brought the answer that he came from Béarn in the Pyrenees. He was probably, the crown prince reported to his friends, delighted and amused at this discovery, a distant cousin.

The secret of King Gustaf's success is to be found in the way in which he has accepted the curtailment of his powers; in other words he is a master of the art of yielding gracefully, yielding without seeming to surrender. As recently as twenty-five years ago the king had the power to form a government of ministers which he himself had chosen. That power is still his in the written Constitution but he would never dream of using it, realizing that such an attempt would not be tolerated. Today he names to office those ministers designated by the party with a working majority in the Riksdag. Thus a profound change has come about in a quarter of a century.

In the expression of a British labor leader, royalty, in Sweden as well as in Great Britain, has become "acclimatized" to democracy. The king stands above political and party strife, receiving those ministers who have a parliamentary majority, regardless of what their brand of politics may be.

There have been times during the past thirty years when this has been none too easy, times when bitterly warring factions sought to swing the balance by bringing the weight of royalty to bear on one side or the other. During the crisis of the general strike of 1909, the whole foundation of Swedish life was shaken. The prestige of the throne would have meant much to the cause of the employers. But one of the leaders of labor was Hjalmar Branting. Hjalmar Branting and King Gustaf had gone to the University of Uppsala together. The king knew and understood Branting and the men he spoke for, and he steadfastly refused to allow the royal name to be used in any way.

What happened during and after the general strike in many ways determined the future. It is an extraordinary segment of labor history, showing what labor can achieve through political action in a democracy. Using political methods to gain a position of power within the state, labor has at the same time strengthened the basis on which democratic government rests.

The real development of the Swedish labor movement began with the formation in 1898 of "L.O.," the Lands-Organisationen. A decade later it had 2,172 locals with 162,391 members and an annual income of 4,703,199 kronor. What was even more important, it had made its influence felt throughout the country in various ways. In 1902 L.O. had called a partial "general strike" in connection with the agitation for an extension of the right to vote without regard to property qualifications. One response to this strike was the formation of the Svenska Arbetsgifvareföreningen or Swedish Employers Association.

The two camps were thus openly intrenched and it became apparent that sooner or later they would clash. Again in 1905 L.O. threatened a general strike, this time to aid in enforcing a peaceful settlement of the crisis that followed Norway's demand for independent statehood. Labor's threat, it is agreed, played no small part in the pacific termination of this quarrel. It was in September of 1905 that the employers' organization adopted "paragraph 23," which, in effect, pledged each member to maintain an open shop and to submit all collective wage agreements entered into with workers to the officers of the organization for final approval. A year later an agreement was reached with L.O. which provided that "the right to organize shall not be restricted by either side," and that "if any workers feel that they have been discharged under such circumstances that a violation of the right to organize may seem to have occurred, they have a right to ask for an investigation through their organization before other measures are taken." But for all that this was a concession, the battle lines were more sharply drawn.

With the depression that began in 1907 there were numerous strikes. Employers sought to reduce wages that were already low. The bitter struggle of the workers is vividly described in Gösta Larsson's *Our Daily Bread*. Organized capital felt that the time had come to break the power of organized labor. Once more labor was drawn to the idea of the general strike, remembering how effective the threat had been in 1902 and 1905.

On July 14, 1909, the employers' organization sent an ultimatum to leaders of L.O. that unless all strikers were back at work by July 26 all L.O. workers would be locked out, regardless of whether they had participated in the strikes. The answer to this was an order calling a general strike to begin August 4. A number of local lockouts, as well as strikes, were already effective. On July 26 about 50,000 additional workers were locked out and on August 2 another 30,000. Two days later labor showed its power when 150,000 members of L.O. went on strike to be joined by an equal number of nonmembers. Hardly a factory wheel turned in the entire nation. Labor early in the course of the strike was supremely confident of victory.

Leaders of L.O. had been under the influence of Georges Sorel and other French and German Socialist-Laborites. The belief prevailed among Swedish workers that the general strike was an invincible weapon—the inevitable deathblow to capitalism. They had talked for years about how some day they would bend society to their will by the instrument of the general strike. Violence was not necessary to bring about this transformation; they had pledged themselves to abstain from violence. Leaders of L.O. were all for "law and order," lending their support to the temporary prohibition against alcohol that was decreed during the crisis.

The leaders, Hjalmar Branting among them, agreed, too, that the strike should not interfere with sanitation, illumination, water, or the care of the sick. They had assumed that most forms of transportation would be stopped and it was therefore a serious blow when the railroad workers, the majority employed on the state railroads, voted by 15,000 to 7,000 not to join the strike. The railroad employees held with their fellow workers morally but they could not bring themselves to strike against the state; the mails, they felt, must be carried as usual. This, and one other factor, had a great deal to do with the disastrous trend of the strike. While the typographical unions went out, and so effectively that labor's own presses did not function, the employers managed to put their side of the struggle before the public, making full use of the mails and the railroads. In contrast the workers had to rely largely upon speakers and this was long before the day of the radio. Morale began to crumble. The conservatives came out with daily editions, set up by editors and office boys, but black print that damned the strikers as "contract-breakers," revolting against the well-being of the very state itself.

Although there was no violence and labor in the face of starvation and acute suffering held its ranks with perfect order, the conservative government did not hesitate to call out the troops to guard railroad stations and post offices. That, too, was an excellent means of discrediting the strikers. In the industrial areas of Stockholm, Malmö, Göteborg, there was a sharp want of food, clothing, and fuel. The victory that had appeared so certain now seemed further off than at the outset of the strike. And still the forces of labor held almost intact, with an integrity and loyalty that was amazing.

Not until fall merged into winter, the grim northern winter, did the forces of labor weaken. First a formal agreement to return to work was made with employers who were not members of the Arbetsgifvareföreningen, which was responsible for calling the lockout. Then gradually the strike broke down. By December 15 it was all over.

Defeat after the long, despairing struggle was bitter indeed. It was a serious blow to L.O. During the year the movement lost 67,697 members, in 1910 22,905, and in 1911 5,053 more, so that in three years nearly 100,000 dues-paying members dropped out. Likewise the Social-Democratic party fell from a membership of 140,000 to 62,000 and it was ten years before it climbed back to 100,000.

Those who remained have been described as a Roman legion, an irreducible élite. Branting was confident that the employers had won only a Pyrrhic victory and so it has proved to be. Having lost this frontal attack, labor proceeded by slower and more indirect methods to seek power. The leaders of the labor movement launched a long and painstaking campaign of political education. Union headquarters became schools and the labor party, that is the Social-Democratic party, put up candidates for every possible public office. The coöperative societies offered courses in economics, sociology, and history. The A.B.F., or Workingmen's Educational Society, became a kind of labor high school. And Laborites studied above all the technique of winning elections and the subtleties of parliamentary procedure.

Meanwhile the proportional election system had gone into effect in Sweden, and in 1911 the Socialists nearly doubled their membership in the Riksdag, advancing from thirty-five to sixty-four, while the Conservatives dropped from ninety-three to sixty-four. Thus for the first time the Laborites equaled the Right and Liberals replaced Conservatives as the executive party. The trend to the Left has never ceased. Labor party discipline was rigid; on all questions the sixty-four Social-Democrats voted as a solid bloc. All differences of opinion, and there were many, were ironed out in party caucus and not on the floor of the Riksdag. This, too, impressed the public with labor's power and authority.

At the outbreak of the World War, the Social-Democrats used all their influence in behalf of neutrality and they were a significant factor in offsetting the "activists" who favored entrance on the side of Germany. In 1917 when the Liberals returned to power, Hjalmar Branting was a member of the cabinet, evidence of the political growth of the Social-Democrats. Three years later Branting, who had been elected to the Riksdag as the first representative of labor in 1897, was made premier. In eleven years the political battle had been won. This rise of labor after the crushing defeat of the general strike is not without a thrilling quality.

While the Social-Democrats do not have an absolute majority, they have the executive power, and four times they have formed a government. During the past three years they have been successful in collaborating with the Farmers' party. Many costly strikes have occurred since 1920, but L.O. and the employers' organization have learned to respect each other and the method of bargaining between the two camps follows a convenient and familiar pattern. Today there is virtual peace on the labor front. The only recent strike was that of the telegraph linemen against the government Telegraph Board. To the outsider it seems incongruous that government employees should be striking for higher wages against a Socialist government. But to the Swedes this is a perfectly natural phenomenon—the strike is the legitimate resort of all workers in collective bargaining.

To express labor's growth in figures, L.O. on January 1, 1935, had 653,231 members, of whom about 100,000 were women This may be contrasted with less than 50,000 members after the failure of-the general strike in 1909. The Social-Democratic party now has 326,734 dues-paying members and at the last general election, on September 18, 1932, polled 1,013,176 votes.

The present prime minister, Per Albin Hansson, is in many ways typical of his party. He is a quiet, solid-appearing man, stocky and cropheaded, with a small, neat belly. Self-educated, in a sense self-made, he was an editorial writer on the Social-

Democratic paper in Gothenburg before he took office. His salary was scarcely more than $2,000 a year. When he took office and for nearly a year afterwards, he lived with his wife in a two-room flat. From that flat he moved to a five-room house in one of Stockholm's modest garden suburbs. And this is not, it should be added for the benefit of the cynical, merely the gesture of a politician toward his humble constituents. It is the way this man of simple tastes would choose to live under any circumstances.

Meeting him in his plain, high-ceilinged office, furnished in the clean, dignified style of modern Sweden, one is aware at once of the quality of his mind. He is grave, slow moving, patient, and above all he is distrustful of doctrine. On practical immediate problems he can and will talk, always with something keen and trenchant to say. But large issues, the future of peoples, and arbitrary patterns of social and economic change he is reluctant to discuss. He is apt to remind the questioner who would lead him into abstract prophecy of the slogan of the Social-Democratic party.

In Swedish it is: *"Samma möjligheter till trygg levnad inom fäderneslandet för alla som där bygga och bo."* Translated literally, this is: "The same possibilities for living securely within the fatherland for all those who inhabit it." But it has richer connotations in the original. For all our differences, contrary purposes, desires, and ambitions we must all live together in peace and security within the fatherland. Sometimes Per Albin Hansson phrases it in another way but that is always what he wants to say—that internal strife, internal rivalries, shall not menace the essential well-being of any group. Alongside the grandiose pretensions of the average political party, the extravagant promises of vast, radiant new worlds, this sounds simple indeed.

It is, I think, deeply significant that the Social-Democrats alone among major parties resisted Kreuger's millions. The liberal leader, the self-righteous Carl Gustav Ekman, was found to have accepted a secret fund from the match king and he collapsed like a punctured balloon, discrediting his liberal party. Even the Swedish Communists, although in no sense a major party, benefited by Kreuger's largesse, it was disclosed as details of the catastrophe came to light. The Russian Communists were too negligible a group to be considered. But one may be certain that Kreuger did not overlook the political power of the Social-Democrats. He found them incorruptible. And undoubtedly this was one of the factors that swept the party into office following Ekman's collapse. For the Swedes have an inherent honesty. Graft in the administration of government has been all but nonexistent.

Kreuger was an international phenomenon. He was first of all an international financier, playing the international game according to the rules of that game, and only secondly, and in a sense by accident, a Swede. More important, perhaps, he was, it is plain, a megalomaniac; one of those mad men dreaming of world power, identified with his own perverse ego, such as recur through history.

Kreuger's story borders throughout upon the pathological, and it is significant that the best analysis of his career has been written by a psychiatrist in his native land. If it is impossible to discover the secret of his strange personality, to penetrate very far beyond his curious, masklike face, it has also been impossible thus far to get at certain more tangible secrets of his career. One thing is evident: the whole story of the Kreuger debacle has not been told and may never be told.

Briefly stated, the truth is that Kreuger in arranging monopolies and loans with the governments of the world dealt of necessity in bribery. In the course of several transactions he had printed upon his own presses in Stockholm the bonds of other governments, bonds that were recognized subsequently as authentic and with the authentic signatures of the heads of these governments. The "proof" of the forgery of the Italian bonds rests upon very slight evidence. There is involved in this issue the delicate question of international relationships, transcending all ordinary courts.

But what is even more mysterious is the relationship between Kreuger and the Wallenbergs, in particular old Knut Wallenberg. And yet there emerges the outline, the shadowy shape, of an irreconcilable conflict between these two great capitalists, so dissimilar in every respect.

Kreuger's internationalism was opposed to all that the Wallenberg family and the Wallenberg name have stood for during three generations. He was, to begin with, an interloper who without so much as a by-your-leave invaded the domain of high finance that the Wallenbergs had dominated for so long. The fellow had no background. His father was nothing but a small match manufacturer. He was an adventurer, a queer fish. But what was even more damning, he did not play the game according to the rules. He did not respect the orthodox powers on the international chessboard or concede to them any share of the financial empire that he was creating. Leaping over tariff barriers, he defied the "rights" of the traditional powers and dealt in terms of millions with governments themselves.

In contrast the Wallenberg fortune, in finance and international trade, is built upon a sound and conservative basis, with a deep respect for the great international bankers who control world commerce. This Kreuger talked some new crazy kind of internationalism, an economic world state, made up of moonshine and hollow hopes. So it must have appeared to hardheaded old Knut Wallenberg. And yet the Wallenbergs accorded Kreuger a kind of coöperation. He was too big to ignore.

What actually happened at the end no one may ever know. Desperate for cash, Kreuger had pledged with J. P. Morgan & Company the shares of one of the most valuable properties in his financial empire—the Swedish firm, L. M. Ericsson Company, manufacturers of telephone apparatus for most of Europe, with exclusive contracts in many instances to furnish such equipment. It has been printed in one of the Kreuger biographies that a confidential representative of the Morgan bank talked to Kreuger on the morning of March 13, 1932, telling the match king point-blank that the "forgery" was known and suggesting that the only thing left was suicide. That night or the following morning, according to this biographer, Kreuger shot himself.

One may only hope that the definitive biographer will be able to draw upon more complete materials. For Kreuger's life has a place, and not a small place either, in any account of the collapse of internationalism, financial and political.

At eighty-two Knut Wallenberg shows no signs of decadence. There are two views of this tough old man. In one view he is a national hero, the sturdy oak of Swedish finance. He leads a life of almost Spartan simplicity. His views on the primary virtues are respectfully printed in the conservative press. The Wallenbergs, in this generous view, are content to derive their profit, or the greater part of it, from foreign trade, impelled by the motives of deepest loyalty and patriotism. Their interests both at home and abroad are, of course, extremely diverse.

The other view, as dark as this is light, is current among the mass of the people. The ancient head of the family is represented as a financial pirate, with the inherited traits of his forbears who, according to legend, were actual sea pirates. The influence of the Wallenbergs is looked upon as sinister and all pervasive, dominating the financial and industrial life of the country, opposed to all progress and reform. Labor and the cooperatives have had to fight the family every step of the way. The clan Wallenberg has resisted change as bitterly and as fiercely as the capitalists in any other country, if one may believe the leaders of labor. Victories have come only out of struggle.

The old man is now a somewhat remote figure, all his great battles behind him. As Minister for Foreign Affairs in the critical period from February of 1914 to March of 1917, he performed an extraordinary service in preserving Sweden's neutrality despite strong forces that would have drawn Scandinavia into the war. There was a determined pro-German element among the upper classes and particularly in the court, centering about the late queen. Tireless patience and perseverance were required to thwart this influence which grew in strength so long as a German victory seemed possible.

During recent years there has been increasing evidence that the Wallenbergs would like to stand in the good graces of their countrymen. The clan, and especially old Knut, have made numerous gifts to Sweden. But they are never long in favor. Recently Marcus Wallenberg announced that he was moving his legal residence from Stockholm into the country nearby in order to escape high taxes in the city. A storm of protest broke, in the course of which all the old accusations were revived. It raged for weeks in the liberal and labor press. Not one public virtue was conceded to any member of the family, so sharp was the anger aroused by Marcus Wallenberg's flight.

The deepest source of the elder Wallenberg's pride is his contribution to Stockholm's Town Hall. From time to time he gave large sums of money but, too, he brought to the building of the Town Hall an intense interest that extended to the smallest details. And dominating and possessive although he is said to be, he seems to have understood the true nature of the Town Hall.

If any modern building has risen out of the desires and hopes and beliefs of a people, in the sense that a great cathedral represented the aspirations of a particular place and a particular time beautifully and sharply focused, it is Stockholm's Town Hall. The past and present are fused in it, the swelling Byzantine shapes that came out of the East by way of Russia and the strong, simple masses of present day architecture. And the whole is harmonious. In the same way, it seems to me, there is a balance in modern Swedish life, between the past, all that was elemental in the life of a primitive sea-faring people, and the present, the machine, the complexity of modern civilization. It is not "perfect" in the sense of the "perfection" of architecture in the functional style. The latter has achieved a simplicity that is arbitrary and devoid of human values; a simplicity that is a kind of desperate refuge from the fearful complexity of the present day. One may pick "flaws" in the Town Hall; one may quarrel over details. For after all it did evolve out of the minds of men, not without conflict; the pride and above all the jealousy, the intense jealousy, of planners, architect, designers, painters, sculptors, craftsmen, have gone into it. But it is a complete expression of a time and a people and it has, if only for this reason, a rare nobility.

The mass of it, a glowing ruddy color, rises above Lake Mälar like a red granite cliff. The eye follows the tower to the light, open cupola and the three golden crowns that top it. It is the heart of the city and all the life of the town flows in and around it. There is the sense that it might have been hewn centuries ago out of the rock of the island on which it stands, but a feeling, too, that one will return to it again and again, as to something never really old.

Ragnar Östberg, the architect of the Town Hall, submitted his first plan in a national competition in 1893. Through the years he gathered around him a notable group of designers, sculptors, painters, craftsmen, and as the project took definite form, they became more and more absorbed in it, dedicating themselves to its realization. When, after the final political difference had been composed and the funds had been made available, actual construction began, Östberg and his aides went to live on the site of the building so that they might at all times watch its growth. And when, during the war, it seemed that there would not be enough money to complete the roof in copper, as originally specified, hundreds of citizens of Stockholm came forward and contributed $6 for every copper plate. On each copper shingle was a number and opposite that number in a great book was recorded the name of the donor.

It was completed in 1923 and dedicated at a great national celebration on the four-hundredth anniversary of Gustavus Vasa's coronation. Every phase of the Swedish temperament finds expression in the rich variety of moods that the Town Hall displays. In the Blue Hall there is the light color, the clear, sunny warmth, that is the deep-rooted desire of the northerner through the stubborn, interminable winter; the longing for the south that is almost a racial nostalgia. The Golden Chamber has a barbaric splendor that is reminiscent of the Vikings. In the inner court, with the deeply recessed windows and the Byzantine turrets thrust up against the skyline, one is aware of the sure, slow strength of the people who built the Town Hall— as though it had been a fortress against the attacks of those who would weaken the ancient fiber of their race.

With one or two exceptions, the most unfortunate being Carl Milles, the sculptor, every important artist and craftsman contributed to the beauty of the Town Hall. Not only the sculptures in the formal garden and the murals on the walls, but the light chandeliers, the draperies, the furniture, the rugs, received the loving care of men and women distinguished in their respective fields in Sweden. It was a signal honor to be called upon to contribute some detail, however minor, to the completed whole.

Sweden's renascence of the arts began before the World War and had a rapid growth from 1920 to 1925. Befitting a practical people, it was a renascence in architecture and the applied arts rather than in the fine arts. At the Paris decorative arts exposition in 1925, when the principal awards went to Sweden, the world realized that something significant was happening in the north. Designers and architects employed common materials, pewter, glass, the ordinary Swedish woods, but by their distinguished treatment of these common materials, they endowed them with authority and a simple dignity. The furniture, glassware, pewter, textiles they created were modern in their essential simplicity of line but they had a kinship with the past in ornament, sparingly used, and in wide variety of forms.

Many designers acknowledge their debt to the ancient patterns that have come down through generations of textile weavers and furniture makers. As the shapes of factory-made things took on a new simplicity and beauty under the spur of the Swedish Arts and Crafts Society's program, so did the old handcrafts, and particularly textiles, take a renewed hold on public imagination. This was partly the result of government encouragement, through the support of schools for textile weavers, but it came also out of an æsthetic sense quickened by new and brilliant designs. Modern craftsmen in textiles, such as Elsa Gullberg and Einar Forseth, created exquisite new patterns and revived forms long neglected or forgotten. Because of this union of the old and new, textiles played an important part in the rebirth of Sweden's arts and crafts.

The modest slogan of the Swedish Arts and Crafts Society, "More beautiful things for everyday life," is not unlike that of the Social-Democratic party. There is the same unpretentiousness about it. And yet from 1915 onward it was a rallying cry. The society sought to raise the general level of taste not only by direct propaganda but by convincing manufacturers that the level of public taste demanded better design. Leaders of the society succeeded, and it may have been their most important contribution, in bringing together craftsmen and designers on the one hand and manufacturers on the other, persuading them that the arrangement was for their mutual benefit.

The manufacturers, and this was a remarkable achievement, were made to understand the rôle of the designer and the place that must be accorded to him if he was to be effective. Many designers, such as Hald and Gate in glass, Ivar Johnsson in wrought iron, Fougstedt in pewter, Elsa Gullberg in textiles, became an important part of the businesses in which they engaged. This partnership between business and the arts served greatly to advance the cause of Vackrare Vardagsvara, "More beautiful things for everyday life."

No one can doubt that the influence of the Swedish Arts and Crafts Society has altered the taste of every level of the population. It has done much to sweep away the heritage of nineteenth-century stuffiness and the atrocities of *l'art nouveau*. This does not mean that the interior of every workman's flat is a mean between Corbusier and Elsie de Wolff. But light, space, simplicity and bright color have replaced to a surprising extent the heavy, crowded, dark flats of two or three decades ago.

In the rebirth of the arts and crafts that occurred in Sweden from 1915 to 1930 it is difficult not to see a clear relationship to the harmony and well-being of the country's social and political life. I am familiar with the thesis that art comes out of ferment and unrest, but that is, perhaps, art on another and higher level. Sweden's renascence is that of a people who seem singularly well adjusted to living; a rebirth of the art of living. Functionalism, the international style, has made headway among the younger architects, and there are some excellent examples of this style, particularly the public library that Asplund did for Stockholm. But it is too arbitrary, too rigid in its exclusion of everything that has gone before, ever to take a deep hold in Sweden.

In their ability to choose what they will preserve and what they will discard from out of the past lies undoubtedly one of the sources of the wisdom of the Swedes, in small things as in great. They abolished the House of Nobles because it was merely obstructive, devoid of any real relationship to the present, a reform which the Labor party in Great Britain is trying belatedly to carry out against the House of Lords. They have preserved the king as a living flag, a symbol of the nobility of the state.

Formerly each year when the question of the appropriation for the royal family came up in the Riksdag, the Left, Social-Democrats, Communists, and Liberal Republicans had a field day of oratory in which they denounced royalty and all its works in the strongest terms. In particular, one Communist in the Parliament, Ture Nerman, was given to language of violent denunciation. He is the mildest of men in his personal life, a poet and an intellectual. At the end of one of Nerman's vehement speeches on the crown, Mauritz Hellberg, a veteran Liberal member of Parliament, rose to reply.

"I've listened to many speeches on the crown," Hellberg said, "and I've made many myself, advocating the abolition of the crown. But I think our bloodthirsty friend goes a little too far. The king is like Santa Claus. We know when he puts on that red robe and that high crown that he is just one of us, but we like to see him dress up in those fine clothes."

Here was pragmatic wisdom, the power of the symbol expressed in simplest terms. The Riksdag voted the appropriation for the crown as it had always done and as it will in all probability continue to do for many years to come. The annual appropriation for the households of the king and the crown prince is slightly more than 800,000 kronor, the smallest item in a budget of more than a billion crowns. It is not, one is told by the thrifty Swedes, a very costly luxury, this human flag, this king.

X

DENMARK ORGANIZES THE FARM

THE metamorphosis that occurred in Denmark in the half century from 1880 to 1930 is nothing short of miraculous. The fortunes of this small country were at the lowest ebb in the decade after 1865. The people themselves were in a state of abject misery and apathy that was close to utter despair. Prussia and Austria had administered the final humiliation in 1864 when they had made war upon Denmark that ended with the loss of Schleswig, a province in which 200,000 Danes lived. In a country reduced to scarcely half the size of Maine, with very limited mineral resources, the soil, impoverished by centuries of misuse, was tilled by peasants who were little better than serfs attached to the great feudal estates. Denmark was actually on the verge of national disintegration.

But already, even before this point of extreme despair had been reached, the forces destined to recreate the land were at work. That extraordinary national hero, Bishop Nicholas Frederik Severin Grundtvig, had through his teaching prepared the way for a new epoch. Not long after his death, in 1872, the first results of the doctrines he had spread abroad began to be apparent.

Grundtvig preached a kind of nationalism new to Europe. He stirred the mass of the people to a sense of their common heritage, their common language and literature, the glory of the past. What he did, essentially, was to prepare the way for a strong national government that would direct the economic and social life of the country. This was his first major contribution. Second, he taught the Danes coöperation; he showed them a practical way to rebuild their nation. And he schooled them above all in the use of the instruments of democracy, political and economic.

Perhaps the most important instrument that he gave them was the unique educational form known as the Danish folk high school—a school for adults that should be intimately allied with rural life. The new school was to teach the people to know the Danish background and to understand and appreciate their heritage. But even more important; it was to instruct them in practical methods for drawing the most from the life in which they found themselves. They were to learn not only how to make more money through farming, but the pleasures of singing and dancing and reading; not on some remote plane in some stratum of existence to which they might aspire but in their own homes and whenever they gathered together. These schools were to be Danish schools, with no foreign languages such as were considered necessary to the education of the upper classes. In Grundtvig's conception, the teacher would live and work with his pupils, and thereby become a focus for community life.

While Grundtvig was still living the first folk high school was started. A half dozen sons of farmers, young men in their early twenties, studied with Kristen Kold, the first teacher, in an old farm building. From that beginning there has grown the national institution of the folk school. Today there are 2,500 continuation and evening schools for young adults in city and country with more than 60,000 pupils. Of actual folk high schools there are today sixty with a total of 6,400 students.

The folk high schools and the continuation schools are distributed through the whole country. There are courses in ordinary subjects, history, literature, economics, hygiene, but always with stress upon Denmark. And then there are courses in practical subjects, animal husbandry, domestic science, handcrafts, coöperative management. Each individual folk high school is owned by the farmers of the neighborhood in which it is located; the farmers form associations for the support of their school. The course for young men is customarily in the winter, from November to May, while young women take a three-month course in the summer. The fees, including board and lodging under a common roof, are about $20 a month. For students who could not otherwise attend school the government provides the fee; it maintained 3,500 pupils through grants of tuition in the year 1932–33.

As an indication of the influence these schools have had, it is estimated that at least one third of the present farming population has taken courses at some time during the past thirty years. Education and coöperation were the two great forces at work for the rebirth of Denmark. Behind Bishop Grundtvig's rallying cry, "All for one and one for all," was the slow realization by the body of the people of how they might recreate their common lot. At the same time there began a fundamental change in the land system, and it was this basic economic change that made it possible for the people to progress through education and coöperation.

Although serfdom was abolished in Denmark in 1788, the large estates, tilled under a system of paid agricultural labor, persisted up until the middle of the last century, and the estate owners had certain privileges which they exercised until lately. The land was leased by comparatively few owners on extremely harsh terms to a large tenant class. But about 1850 certain public-spirited individuals began a movement to enable tenants to borrow money at low interest rates. Many tenants took advantage of these rates and soon demonstrated that farming on a small scale by individual owners was far more profitable than the tenant system. The superiority of the new method was so obvious that even the estate owners were compelled to acknowledge it, and they were therefore more willing to part with lands their families had held for centuries.

As a part of the general awakening that was to transform the entire country, another land movement came into being. It was incorporated in 1866 as the Danish Heath Society. While the society had an excellent leader in Colonel E. M. Dalgas, it was not slow in enlisting widespread support so that it, too, might be considered a popular movement. As with education and coöperation, it was not superimposed reform but a determined effort at self-regeneration that made the Heath Society a powerful force in Danish life.

The society proposed to reclaim barren land and to reforest areas stripped by improper forestry—it was an imperative need with rich Schleswig gone and the remaining population largely dependent upon agriculture, both for consumption and export. The Heath Society has carried its program to every part of the country, draining the land, cultivating bogs and meadows, planning irrigation projects, building roads, converting waste marshes into fertile fields. From the beginning the heath farmers themselves—there are nearly 14,000 paid up memberships today—have done most of the work, but always under the expert guidance and advice of the society.

The work began in Jutland where prior to 1860 there were 4,500 square miles of uncultivated land, nearly three fourths of which has been restored. Jutland has been transformed, literally, from a wasteland to a pleasant, profitable farming area. With success in Jutland, the activities of the Heath Society were greatly enlarged and directed toward the reclamation of other submarginal regions. Rivers were straightened and the height and volume of their flow controlled; this rendered bordering marshes and lowlands arable. In three years the society completed eighty miles of irrigation canals, freeing thousands of acres of sour and stagnant water. Dikes were constructed, and under the direction of the society many square miles of barren land were treated with fertilizers. Altogether it is estimated that the amount of arable land in Denmark has been increased by more than 20 per cent through the efforts of the Heath Society. And the total forest area has been increased from 6 per cent to 9 per cent which represents more of a triumph than appears on the surface, since the forests have been made to yield a considerable supply of timber.

Support for the work of the Heath Society has come not alone from the farmers who stand to benefit most by it, but from several other sources. The state has each year provided a generous subsidy. Far more remarkable is the fact that large numbers of city dwellers in every rank of society have become contributing members and have taken a keen and active interest in the society's program. A considerable number of bequests have come from both farm and city members to aid the work. It is obvious that there is a general realization that Denmark's well-being rests upon agriculture. This is a kind of nationalism, a national consciousness, that transcends certain of the class, sectional, and occupational antagonisms prevailing in continental countries such as the United States; and along with it goes the knowledge that the very existence of the nation depends upon a large degree of coöperation, even at a real sacrifice, between classes, sections, and persons of various occupations.

The movement to parcel out the estates into small individually owned holdings had gained such force that by 1899 the first of several land allotment laws was passed. Under the terms of this law the government is authorized to lend to a prospective purchaser in advance a sum equal to nine tenths of the purchase price of the land as shown on the registered title. In addition, if there are roofed-in buildings on the land, the purchaser can borrow, with the approval of local officials, up to one third of their value. These loans are secured by a government mortgage on the entire property and this mortgage cannot be foreclosed so long as the purchaser puts the lands to the uses stipulated in the law.

Provisions for repayment are extremely liberal. Interest on loans on land is at the rate of 4½ per cent and the same rate applies on building loans. No part of the principal is repaid during the first five years of the loan. And after this five-year period the borrower pays only small annual installments, equivalent to 1 per cent of the total building loan, until he has paid back the portion that is interest free. The loan on the land is finally redeemed by annual payments in which both interest and amortization are equivalent to 5½ per cent of the original amount of the loan.

A careful study of each applicant and the land that he hopes to buy is made by the government. The question of whether or not the farmer will be able to run his new farm on a profitable basis and repay his loan is one which the government seeks to answer first of all. Not only the applicant's financial standing, but his character and the esteem in which he is held in the neighborhood are considered in arriving at an answer. It is true, however, that those applicants who have put by sufficient savings to meet the interest requirements on the loan in the early years are given preference.

The law of 1899 was broadened in 1919 in such a way that the government was given authority to take over large areas of land in those districts where the small purchaser could not buy at all or where the land was held at a price that was inequitable. Needless to say this greatly enlarged the scope of the program. At the outset under this new legislation the government acquired 85,000 acres, sufficient for about 5,000 small holdings.

The way in which purchases are made under the new law is very interesting. It is scarcely a purchase at all. The farmer desiring to acquire a small holding pays down no purchase money whatsoever, merely contracting with the government to make an annual interest payment equal to about 4½ per cent of the value of the land. The valuation of the land is determined periodically by a committee of government experts. The government will loan to the "purchaser" nine tenths of the cost of suitable farm buildings, with interest at the rate of 4½ per cent up to 8,000 kroner, roughly $2,000, and no interest charge above that level. The building loans may be repaid on the same liberal terms as under the earlier law.

With the government as landlord, under the provisions of the liberalized law, it became possible for a farm hand with one tenth of the sum necessary for building a house and barns, together with a small working capital for livestock and tools—say as little as $300—to set himself up as an independent farmer. The state reserves the right to take back the land if it is "sold" to any other than the direct heir of the original "purchaser." It is significant of the success of the land program that this has been necessary in only a negligible number of cases. Under the law of 1899 nearly 11,000 small farms with individual owners were established, the government advancing $23,000,000 in loans and subsidies. From 1920 to 1932 approximately 6,000 small holdings were acquired by individuals through government aid. And the government has spent nearly $25,000,000 in the acquisition of lands from owners of large tracts since 1920.

As with most of the changes that have come about in Scandinavia, the government has been but one agent, one factor, in the success of this fundamental reform. Perhaps equally important has been the part played by private "parceling out associations" formed under the law of 1899. These associations were formed to assist prospective purchasers in the selection of farms and in raising the necessary loans. There are about twenty such associations. The largest of them has bought more than

125 large estates which have been parceled out into nearly 2,000 small farms; in addition, out of the 125 estates, this association has sold hundreds of acres to the government. Another large association has been instrumental in establishing more than a thousand new farms. If the Ministry of Finance has approved the rules of these associations, they may borrow funds from the government to carry on their work, the estates to be parceled out serving as collateral. In this way they have been able to extend their program very rapidly.

The phrase "small holding" in Denmark means small indeed according to American standards. The bulk of the small farms established under the land program are from nine to thirty-seven acres in size. And nearly 45,000 of these farms are from one acre to nine acres. The latest figure shows that less than 7 per cent of all farms are farmed by tenants.

Holdings as small as these require farming of an intensity that is almost comparable with that of Japan. And, as the Danes are proud to acknowledge, they call for the closest coöperation. Agriculture in Denmark prior to the depression achieved the highest level of prosperity and efficiency in the world by virtue of coöperation and the most thorough education in scientific farming. And Denmark was able to send her agricultural products abroad to compete successfully in a half dozen markets because the profit of the middleman and the processor was largely eliminated.

The coöperative movement in Denmark grew directly out of the folk education that was Bishop Grundtvig's bequest to his people. Today 90 per cent of the Danish farm population is formed into one great coöperative which is the heart of the economic life of the country. There are 5,000 coöperative societies, consumer, marketing and credit, and they are united in the Federated Danish Coöperative Association which is in turn directed by the Central Coöperative Council. At the peak of prosperity their business approached a total of two billion kroner, $250,000,000. This sum may be measured against a total population of slightly more than three and a half millions.

It was by force of necessity, when America in the 'seventies invaded the world wheat market with the bountiful harvests of the newly opened prairies, that Denmark revised her entire agricultural system, turning to dairy products, eggs and bacon. The Danish Coöperative Egg Export Association was formed in 1880. The first coöperative creamery was established in 1881. Today there are more than 1,500 such creameries. Denmark furnished one third of all the butter in the world market and 90 per cent of it came out of these coöperative dairies. Of 210,000 Danish farms, 190,000 hold memberships in coöperative dairies. Coöperative credit societies and banks sprang up very rapidly and were of notable assistance in the land program.

By 1890, 700 dairying coöperatives had been formed. Processed coöperatively, the output of these dairies was sent abroad through coöperative butter exporting societies. It was possible for the small farmer through his coöperative to dispose of his milk supply at the same price as that obtained by the large-scale dairy farmer. Under coöperation, too, the market for dairy products was kept far more stable than it had ever been before.

It was in 1887 that the first bacon factory was started. Today there are fifty-eight with an annual turnover, according to the latest figures, of nearly $100,000,000. Here, too, Bishop Grundtvig's text, "All for one and one for all," was proved in practical gains to coöperating farmers. By virtue of their pooled resources, Danish coöperators were able to advertise the real superiority of Danish bacon throughout the continent, and particularly in Great Britain. In this way a stable demand was created. Today all the factories are organized in the Union of Danish Coöperative Bacon Factories for the protection of their common interest.

Coöperation has invaded every phase of agricultural life. A coöperative society of seed growers markets its output, with a guarantee of quality. This group makes its sales largely through the Coöperative Wholesale Society of Denmark. Cattle export has also been organized coöperatively; in 1932 there were fifteen societies with 14,000 members. In the egg export association virtually all poultry farmers are concentrated, supplying those carefully labeled eggs that reach London breakfast tables with such dispatch.

Fertilizers and feed stuffs and grain are purchased on a coöperative basis through societies that are closely allied with the marketing groups. Four large purchasing organizations had an annual turnover prior to the depression of more than $25,-000,000. Farmers, as would be expected, form the bulk of the consumer coöperative societies. The Danish farmer may buy and sell within his own coöperative system, a system so complete that virtually none of the money he spends goes into private profit; nor has the income that he receives been depleted by the levies of a private processor or middleman.

At every turn the government has helped the coöperatives to improve the quality of agricultural products. There are twenty-one agricultural schools in Denmark and each has created a model farm that serves as a splendid object lesson to small farmers in the district in which the college is situated. What is more, these model farms are made to pay their own way. There exists a remarkable liaison between the farm and the agricultural college so that the scientific methods of the latter become part of the small farmer's knowledge and background, a knowledge readily applied to the farmer's immediate problems.

One of the most important factors in bringing about this working understanding between science and the farmer has been the control societies established to enable the dairyman, large or small, to know precisely the economic value of each cow that he owns and to compare this with the ranking of the cows owned by his neighbor. These societies now have their own experts who visit all farms regularly and make thorough tests every two weeks. The results of these tests are entered in uniform record books which are kept by control societies in every district. Today there are nearly 1,500 such societies and almost a half million cows are inspected. From the government the societies get an annual subsidy of $35,000 which is distributed by the Minister of Agriculture.

But the government, although it has extended aid to agriculture in various forms, readily acknowledges the achievement of the coöperatives. And it is careful to point out that the position of the coöperatives was achieved without subsidies or appreciable assistance of any kind. In short, out of a common need there grew this remarkable collective enterprise.

On the example of the folk schools various community groups have been formed; athletic clubs, reading circles, singing societies and large folk meetings; hundreds of people gathered on a holiday afternoon under a pleasant grove of trees to listen to lectures of a broadly cultural nature and to enjoy simple entertainment. This sounds a little deadly. But it is not. For it is infused with the good humor and the gayety of the Danes. It is well to remember that they have built the most attractive amusement park in the world, Tivoli in Copenhagen, which last year had its centennial celebration with a visit from the prime minister and all his cabinet.

Many of the folk high schools have become very well known and educators from all over the world have come to observe their methods. The oldest and most famous of the schools is that of Askov in Jutland. Peter Manniche's International People's College at Elsinore has also gained a world-wide reputation. But though they have become well established, famous even, the folk schools are run on the simple plan that their founder originally conceived. The teachers live with their pupils and share their lives, participating in the life of the community. And they are, as Bishop Grundtvig believed they would be, leaders and counselors of the people. It is interesting to note that the Swedes adapted the idea of the folk high school to their own practical temperament. In Sweden the folk high schools are more often affiliated with trade schools.

It is not to be wondered at that this socialized education has produced advanced social laws, pertaining to women and children, public health, the hours and conditions of labor. Denmark's pioneer laws have had such a wide influence that it is scarcely necessary even to mention them here. Less well known is the fact that the Danes have built a thorough and scientific tax structure which includes a levy upon the capital value of property, intended to relieve land of a disproportionate burden and to defray the cost of advanced social services. It must also be realized that a very small share of the Danish budget goes to military defense.

If all this has the air of a latter-day Arcady, yes, of Utopia, it is because the Danes actually did achieve a very high type of rural civilization. The civilization was based upon the export of agricultural produce in open competition in the world market. But what has happened to agricultural prices during the depression is all too well known. Furthermore the trade in agricultural products has felt the direst effects of economic nationalism.

The Beaverbrook newspapers in England cried out against Danish bacon and Danish butter and eggs. They were undermining British prosperity, destroying the very fiber of British statehood. A political government responded with increased tariffs and complicated trade agreements. Germany put drastic restrictions on food imports. Danish farmers through their cooperatives have used every resource to meet these national reprisals but they have felt keenly nevertheless the cruel force of the depression. And they have demanded, as farmers the world over have demanded, that the government act to raise farm prices. In a country the size of Denmark, where agriculture is so largely dependent upon the world market and where the trade balance is built upon farm products, such artificial price manipulation as the Roosevelt administration has attempted is plainly out of the question.

In the late summer of 1935, 50,000 farmers gathered in the courtyard of the palace in Copenhagen in an extraordinary demonstration to which the king responded with a personal appeal for loyalty. There are conflicting reports about this demonstration. Parties of the Left charged that it was engineered by the Nazis as a threat against the Social-Democratic government and certainly there were many Nazi sympathizers among the demonstrators. But in part it appears to have been a nonpolitical demonstration of farmers dependent upon the export of butter, eggs, and bacon, in protest against the tariff on grains and hay, raw materials which these farmers in large part must import. No demonstrators, according to observers, came to Copenhagen from districts in which grain and hay are still the principal crops.

A part of the continent, Denmark has always been more involved in European politics than Sweden. Inevitably this has been so and Denmark has suffered bitterly in the past for her proximity to Germany. Nazi Germany now looks with covetous eyes on the territory that went to Denmark by plebiscite at the close of the World War.

Consumers' coöperatives and state ownership and operation of monopolies have played a vital part in Danish economy, as in Sweden. But what the Danes have done to remodel agriculture stands out as a unique achievement. It is one that has been often described but it seemed worth while to summarize it here if only because of the great influence it has exerted upon Sweden.

XI

RECOVERY

SWEDEN'S recovery has been one of the most remarkable phenomena of the depression. The index of industrial production rose to 104 in November, 1934, with 1929 as 100, and a high level was sustained through 1935. For the same month the index of employment reached 98, using the average for the years 1925 to 1930 as 100. In August of 1935 the unemployed totaled only about 43,000 persons, considerably less than 1 per cent of the entire population. In Stockholm there were actually less than 4,000 unemployed. Foreign trade increased throughout the entire year. And there were other even more tangible proofs of recovery. The sale of wine, an infallible barometer, mounted rapidly. An increasing number of licenses for radio receivers were issued. More telephones were installed than ever before.

Through August and September of 1935 the revenue from automobile licenses was up and the rate of consumption of electric power was rising. In many districts taxes have been paid up to 95 per cent. There has been a building boom which began with the end of the building trades strike of 1934. Several mortgage banks and industrial concerns have been able to float bonds at 3 per cent and no government issue now convertible pays more than 3½ per cent. In fact, the cautious Swedes are concerned for fear that this mild boom will get out of hand.

Another significant fact is the successful balancing of the budget for 1935–36, with no extraordinary expenditures for the relief of unemployment or public works. The budget for the fiscal year of 1935–36 was balanced at 1,065,000,000 kronor which with the crown at the old parity with the dollar, where it was in the spring of 1935, is approximately $250,000,000. There was a small budgetary surplus in 1935 due to greatly increased tax yields. And in 1936–37 an active program of debt retirement was initiated as the result of a large budgetary surplus.

It is significant, too, that the estimates on which the latest budget is based include substantial gains from state-owned industries, which, according to early returns, are almost certain to be realized. The Royal Board of Waterfalls puts the surplus revenue from the state's utility system at approximately $5,000,-000 for the current fiscal year. The income from the telegraph and telephone systems is listed at about $8,000,000 in the budget forecast. The state railways are expected to yield more than $6,000,000. The Royal Board of Forestry is expected to pay into the Treasury nearly $3,000,000 in revenue from the state forests. The capable managers of these state industries are not merely guessing at the amounts of these surpluses; they have a sound basis in past experience for predicting increased activity which will in turn increase their revenues.

The reasons for Sweden's recovery are as diverse as the nature of her economic life. Fortuitous circumstances—fortuitous for Sweden at least—quite beyond domestic control have contributed a great deal to recovery. Without certain developments in world trade and world politics that worked greatly to Sweden's advantage recovery would never have been so far advanced. But it is true that because Sweden's internal economy was well ordered she was able to make the greatest use of these fortunate turns.

First of all there was the vital increase in the trade in timber with England. And this grew in part out of Great Britain's differences, both political and economic, with Soviet Russia. At the time that timber agreements with Russia were broken off Swedish exporters got large contracts that have been an all important factor in this industry which is basic to Sweden's industrial life.

The European war scare has kept Swedish munitions plants operating on boom time schedules, producing armaments for export. It is not difficult to imagine what this boom has meant to the country's iron and steel plants. The Bofors plant, largest munitions works, has been operating at full capacity for at least five years.

From the point of view of her export trade, Sweden left the gold standard at a most fortunate time, following the example of England in 1931. For several years Sweden had an export advantage over those countries that stayed on gold, an advantage which has remained of tangible value, in so far as the European gold bloc countries are concerned, down almost to the present time.

Sweden is credited by economists with being the first country to attempt to stabilize its currency, not with regard to gold or foreign exchange but in relation to the internal purchasing power of its own money. Retail prices and wages had not fallen as much as the wholesale price level, with the result that the gap between wholesale and retail prices was extremely wide. One of the first objectives of the government in managing the currency was to close this gap so that production might be more profitable to the farmer. Most observers agree that while the move to raise the wholesale level has not been markedly successful, the government has been able to hold the retail price level relatively stable. As early as 1928 the government undertook to restore agriculture to a more profitable basis. This attempt, involving mild quota restrictions in relation to exports and imports of agricultural produce, bears a slight resemblance to the experiments of the Agricultural Adjustment Administration at Washington. But they were not as drastic nor were they predicated upon an economy of scarcity.

The mysteries of currency manipulation are so profound that only a few seers and soothsayers may penetrate them and what they report is for the most part contradictory, abstruse and all too often quite unintelligible. What Sweden achieved through her managed currency was long a matter for debate but of late one has heard very little of currency management. There is a general realization that it is at present playing a minor part in Sweden's recovery.

It is enough to say that there has been a marked degree of monetary stability throughout the depression. The Bank of Sweden has followed a consistent policy, publicly announced. The relation between the pound sterling and the krona has been practically unchanged for several years and in 1934 the relation of the krona to the dollar tended to be more stable. This stability has worked to the great advantage of Swedish exporters. They have been able to make their plans over a definite length of time with reasonable security against disastrous day-to-day fluctuations. The price swing has been comparatively slight. Wholesale prices in Sweden, as in Great Britain, increased 5 per cent from 1932 to the end of 1934, in contrast with an increase of 20 per cent in the United States and 8 per cent in Canada and a decline in the gold bloc countries. The retail price index varied only five points in a period of six years from 1930 to 1936.

Sweden's consistent low tariff policy, maintained throughout the depression, is credited by many with contributing to her recovery. No exchange restrictions were imposed although all over the world other nations were resorting to import quotas and similar devices impeding the flow of trade. On some important products Swedish duties are now the lowest in the world. This is true, for example, of automobiles. And it may well be the reason why imports from the United States increased in 1934 by 78 per cent, the largest trade gain for a single country that America recorded in that year.

Technicians have contributed not a little to the continuing flow of Sweden's foreign trade by improving the products that Sweden has sent into world competition. Swedish steel in a highly refined form goes into Pittsburgh. It is a source of pride that Swedish ball bearings are a part of the mechanism which for five years will continuously grind the lens of the greatest telescope in the world. Recently a leading technician in the wood-pulp field announced that this industry had reached the quantitative limit of expansion and that future growth would have to depend upon bettering the product sent into the channels of world trade.

This technical proficiency has its base in Sweden's universal education. Illiterates constitute less than one tenth of 1 per cent of the population, but this is only a crude measure. Technical schools have reached a high degree of development and they are open to every class, with the competition for places extremely keen. In literature and art most of the first rate younger men and women are sons and daughters of workers who have been educated by the state.

With education so widely diffused it is not surprising that the struggle for place is intense. And here the "royal Swedish jealousy" plays a part. When a professorship at Lund or Uppsala becomes vacant, a major conflict ensues which is invariably taken up by the newspapers and the general public.

These factors, having to do with world trade and currency manipulation, have entered into the so-called recovery that most governments have claimed. The question in Sweden is to what degree coöperation, state ownership, state control of monopolies—the modifications of the capitalist structure this book has been concerned with—have contributed toward restoring prosperity; both in sustaining consumer purchasing power and thereby limiting the course of deflation; and through expansion of state activity impossible to private trade by reason of the world paralysis. To answer it with any finality is plainly impossible since so many intangible and disputed elements are involved. But at least one can put down certain sequences that seem to be cause and effect.

Foremost would come Sweden's public works program. This, as a thorough study by an American economist, Professor C. J. Ratzlaff, has shown, is the result of a long background of experience with work relief. To relieve the widespread want that resulted from the prolonged crop failure of the years 1866 to 1869 state relief committees were formed which received funds from state, province and commune and distributed them through a system of subcommittees. "For especially pressed sections the National Parliament relieved the situation by grants for the support of canal, road, bridge, wharf, and other building projects." The method of unemployment relief has undergone a continuous and gradual evolution from that time forward. Very early the Riksdag recognized that unemployment was a national problem to be brought within the administration of the National Board of Trade. By 1907 the government had come to a frank realization that the poor laws were outmoded as a basis for relief and that instead it was the obligation of the state to provide an opportunity for work for all.

With the outbreak of the World War in 1914 the government foresaw that serious unemployment would grow out of the inevitable decline of world trade and there was formed the National Unemployment Commission. At the start it attempted to regulate relations between employer and employee, along lines not unlike those followed by our National Recovery Administration. The commission called in representatives of labor and industry, agreements were fostered between worker and employer to speed production, and employers and farmers were warned to avoid discharging employees whom they could possibly afford to retain. But these functions were incidental to what has always been the principal task of the commission— relieving unemployment through public works.

The goal of the commission has been a back-log of public works that will absorb the ordinary unemployment and which will also be capable of rapid expansion to meet emergency unemployment in periods of depression. The commission from the outset enjoyed wide freedom of action. It established a rate of pay for "reserve work" which was higher than the amount paid in direct cash relief but lower than wages in private industry. The commission claims that this policy has "in a large measure accounted for the fact that the wholesale unemployment in Sweden has been reduced to normal proportions faster than in most of the European countries." The wage policy has undergone two recent modifications, largely as a result of pressure from the Social-Democratic government. First the commission fixed the wage rate at about 15 per cent lower than the normal wage for unskilled labor paid in the corresponding area; under this change, in localities where the wage scale was low the rate paid on "reserve work" tended to approximate the rate paid in agriculture. The work relief bill of 1933 contained a clear declaration for the prevailing wage rate for unskilled labor in the locality in which the project was to be carried out.

The commission claims that except for three periods of severe unemployment, during intervals of world depression, 1914–15, 1921–22 and 1930 onward, "reserve works" have solved the relief problem. Professor C. J. Ratzlaff challenges this claim. He points out the difficulty of maintaining a sufficient volume of "reserve work" through the winter months, particularly during the winters of 1923 and 1924.

Here, briefly, is the way in which Sweden's "reserve work" has operated. The final decision on projects to be undertaken rests with the National Unemployment Commission. The commission has established certain general principles: the work must benefit the state, a commune, or other public body, and must be justified for economic or cultural reasons but must not be such that it would be carried out normally by ordinary means; wages must form a comparatively large proportion of the cost; and it must be possible to start, stop, extend, or restrict the operation in accord with the fluctuations of private employment.

These conditions have been met most readily by various kinds of construction—roads, railways, harbors, power stations, the regulation of water courses for floating timber, land drainage, and forestry. It is obvious that the choice of public projects—that is, projects of direct benefit to the state—is far wider than, say, in the United States where private industry is fiercely jealous of the encroachments of government. There has never been any lack of proposals and for the most part sound proposals. Between October, 1931, and February, 1932, the commission organized seventy-five new major "reserve work" projects.

When a project has been decided upon, the commission draws up a contract with the local body responsible for the scheme. This legally binding contract specifies a number of things. The local body must provide approved working plans, a survey of the site, stone and gravel pits, necessary machinery, supervision, legal and other preliminary work. The commission in return agrees to carry out the project contracted for in accord with the accepted plan and to complete it to the degree required for the relief of unemployment.

The "reserve work" system is, of course, carefully coördinated with the public employment exchanges that are found throughout the country. Workers are placed on relief registers after they have been unable to secure employment. They are chosen from the register for reserve work. Wages ranged, before the policy laid down by the 1933 work relief bill, from about 95 cents to $1.90 a day, with the majority receiving about $1.15 a day. These figures are arrived at by converting the kronor at the parity rate but they represent, on the whole, a greater purchasing power than would equivalent amounts in our currency. The commission has not hesitated to approve projects requiring movements of labor from one locality to another when this has seemed inevitable and the workers required to move have been provided with adequate housing free of charge.

The balance sheet of the Unemployment Commission for the period from July, 1930, to June, 1931, shows that the average cost a man-day of the state reserve works was about $1.90. Of this 4.7 per cent went into central administration, including the whole cost of the commission; 75.8 per cent went for labor costs; 6.3 per cent for management; and the remaining 13.2 per cent for tools, materials, transport of workers, and other costs.

In 1921 there were 21,000 unemployed on reserve work, in 1922, 31,100, and in 1923, 14,700. These are maximum figures for those years. Wherever one goes in Sweden one sees the work of these earlier years. And the communities take a pride in what has been done. The local mayor makes a point of driving the foreign visitor by a round-about road so that he can say, "There is the bridge we built in 1922 with our reserve workers."

But this system could not begin to take care of the large-scale unemployment which began in 1931. The number of the unemployed increased very rapidly through 1932, advancing from 41,595 in February of 1931 to 108,032 in the same month of the following year, as shown by the unemployed register. By January of 1933 the number on the unemployed register had reached the startling total of 189,225. In a country with a population of little more than 6,000,000, this was cause for serious concern. Of this number only 22 per cent were given relief through the reserve work system.

In the spring of 1933 the Social-Democrats in control of the government, with their leader, Per Albin Hansson, as prime minister, proposed a drastic remedy for this crisis of unemployment. Let us, they said, try to restore purchasing power for a year by putting the whole number of the unemployed to work at the union wage level. While there were 186,561 unemployed in March, it was fairly certain that this number would drop with seasonal employment in the spring to about 145,000 and the Social Democrats went forward with a detailed plan to put 130,000 men back at work either through the reserve system or by subsidies to private industry.

This would require about $42,880,000, it was estimated, and the government proposed to raise this large sum through the sale of short-term obligations carrying a guarantee to repay within about six years. To retire these obligations the government would impose new taxes, chiefly inheritance taxes, increasing the then maximum of 20 per cent to 42 per cent, the new maximum to be applied on the largest fortunes where there was no direct heir.

This radical plan caused an immediate protest from the conservatives. The proposed taxation was equivalent to a major capital levy, they said. It was aimed, they hinted, at the patriarch, Knut Wallenberg, who was eighty years old. Should he die within the six-year period, the inheritance tax, together with other taxes, would take more than half of his estate. We have coöperated before, said the capitalists, but not this time—this is too much.

The Social-Democratic unemployment program called forth a new kind of opposition. Many persons on the Right said, in effect: "Now the time has come to unite and put a stop to this process, for you see it menaces private capital in those very fields that have hitherto been reserved, even by the Socialists, for private enterprise." A few capitalists in Sweden had secretly welcomed the German Nazi reaction. Not only traditions and ties but large investments bound them to German capitalism. In this new controversy the conservatives resorted to tactics that they had hitherto considered beneath their dignity.

On May first, 1933, the masses marched, Communists, Socialists, Anarchists, Esperantists, Syndicalists, every Left Wing group under the sun, all with their banners flying, red banners inscribed with brave devices and heroic mottoes. And then there were the trade-union delegations, solid phalanxes of marching men that seemed to go on forever. And meanwhile virtually all industry was at a standstill. The conservative aristocratic Right decided to have its own May Day, a demonstration, like labor's, of prowess and prestige. There were those who suggested that this might be a little absurd, beneath the dignity of aristocrats, but they were overruled. In the great conservative parade counts and countesses and aide-de-camps to the crown prince and aide-de-camps to Prince Eugen and employees of Stockholm's largest department store—not entirely of their own volition, it was said

—marched on behalf of the Right. And in line with them were many, many little individuals who were marching because they felt it was somehow an honor.

There were forebodings in the months of April and May of some radical turn, to the right or left. The conservatives insisted that they would never yield. An eccentric fringe of black shirts had come into existence. Less than a hundred in number, they nevertheless wore the symbol of Fascism and talked loudly of what they would do when they came into power.

When it came to practical strategy the Social-Democrats did not have a sufficient majority in the Riksdag to put over their unemployment plan. This was probably the reason for the stalemate. Then, suddenly, the Socialists effected one of those working compromises that have served as a basis for much of the progress achieved in Sweden in the past two or three decades. For the first time in parliamentary history the Social-Democrats came to a real understanding with the Farmers' party.

To secure this support some concessions had been made. The Social-Democrats agreed that the wage scale paid to the unemployed on relief works should be not the trade-union rate but the average wage paid to unskilled labor in the locality in which the project was to be carried out. Further, the Social-Democrats agreed not to abolish the Unemployment Commission, which was one of the objectives of the original measure. The important thing was that the essential form of the plan was left untouched by the compromise. The conservatives held aloof but their opposition was passive rather than active. And there followed a dramatic session of the Riksdag in which leaders of both Left and Right forswore absolutism. The conservatives renounced Fascist dictatorship and the Social-Democrats renounced Communist dictatorship. This largely removed from the public mind the fear of a radical move from either extreme which illustrates, incidentally, the extraordinary fact that in Sweden a politician is taken at his word.

Before the government's large-scale work relief program could be put into operation, private employment had begun to show a marked improvement. And by the middle of 1934, industry had made such a remarkable recovery that the Unemployment Commission found it possible to curtail those reserve work projects that had been started before the new unemployment program was passed. Thus Sweden was not compelled to undertake the experiment in mass work relief upon which the United States embarked.

But although Sweden was not forced to go through with this courageous experiment in restoring purchasing power, out of more than twenty years of work relief have come certain conclusions as to this means of solving the problem of unemployment. It is by no means a perfect system from any point of view, as Swedish experience has demonstrated. Besides the very serious difficulties of administration, serious even in a nation of the size and coherence of Sweden, there are the major criticisms of organized labor which appear to an objective observer to be more or less unanswerable. Most projects required only unskilled manual labor. Compelled to accept such public employment through the "willingness to work" test, the skilled laborer ran the grave risk of losing his skill, and if he were transported to a project in another locality he was out of touch with the market in which he could sell his skill and in danger of permanently slipping into the rank of the unskilled.

"It seems to me," says Professor Ratzlaff, "that the government has not faced frankly the alternatives which must be accepted: either, on the one hand, fully to admit that public relief works are limited in their usefulness to manual laborers, and therefore, inadequate; or, on the other hand, to extend widely the scope of public works, not only in number but also in kind, so as to give a fuller range of occupational activity."

Sweden's experience with relief by public works, extending back now for more than twenty years, has demonstrated above all, in the interpretation of Professor Ratzlaff, the value of a long and continuous background of social development. Sweden in relieving unemployment during the depression has had the two essentials: an efficient centralized administration in the Ministry of Social Affairs and an equally efficient decentralized supervision in the public employment exchanges. And behind the system of relief is a basic recognition of the government's responsibility, expressed very well in the report of a special parliamentary committee in 1925:

Even should unemployment decrease at different phases of the business cycle, its entire disappearance from modern society is impossible. There will always be a certain group of persons who are unemployed. Obviously the individual suffers equally as much from unemployment and is in just as great need of help whether the total of the unemployed is large or small. It, therefore, follows that the need of unemployment relief activity always exists . . . which can be seen from the last two years, 1923–25, which were of a normal sort.

To define the part that labor has played in Sweden's recovery is especially difficult. If one accepts the view of classical economists that collective wage agreements, fixed for definite periods, interfere in time of depression with essential adjustments in the cost of production, then it would seem that Sweden's industrial structure was indeed handicapped. For collective agreements, entered into by employers and employees, both highly organized, have included more than half of all industrial workers in the country for at least twenty years. These collective agreements have included an increasing proportion of labor and they have been drawn to take in ever larger areas. Of the 580,- 931 workers brought into collective agreement in 1930–1931, 38.5 per cent were within agreements nation-wide in scope, Professor Ratzlaff has shown. The period covered by these agreements has, however, grown progressively shorter. Virtually none exceeding two years in length has been drawn up since 1920.

The legal status of these collective agreements between closely organized groups of employers and employees was defined in a comprehensive law passed in 1928. A Labor Court was established under the law for enforcement of collective agreements and a schedule of fines was established for failure to observe the terms of these agreements. "The general legal principles governing damages hold, but the ordinary judicial procedure of imposing imprisonment in default of payment of a fine is not applied by the Labor Court." The law also provides for Special Arbitrators who act as mediators in labor disputes and report at stated intervals to the Ministry of Social Affairs. Much more discretion is left to the mediator than in the procedure established for labor boards under the NRA, for example. The method of mediation is not prescribed, nor does the law fix a penalty for the group refusing to accept the offices of mediation. The mediator has no authority to restrict labor organizations in the use of the strike as a weapon in collective bargaining, nor to curtail in any way the militancy of the measures labor may take to gain its objectives.

It was not until 1934 that Sweden adopted a state system of unemployment insurance. The reason it came so late was partly the existence of the system of reserve work which absorbed most of the unemployed in normal periods. But largely it was because the labor unions themselves had developed very early a carefully administered program of unemployment benefits. With virtually every trade fully organized, and a wage level higher than any in Europe, it can readily be understood why this has been an important element in unemployment relief. It was shown by a recent survey of the International Federation of Trade Unions at Amsterdam that the per capita wealth of Swedish trade unions is much larger than that of any other European country.

The first organization for unemployment benefits within a trade union was started as early as 1884. The movement was given a large impetus when the Confederation of Trade Unions was formed in 1898. For the decade from 1910 to 1920 the unions were able to keep benefits at a uniform level, averaging from 54 cents to $1.35 a day to union members without work. There are twenty-two benefit societies connected with various national trade-union groups and they paid out in benefits in 1921, for example, about $2,145,150, which was an average of $11.88 per member. In more recent years the benefits paid out have been as follows: in 1929, $618,535; in 1930, $854,184; and in 1931, $1,707,671.

Denmark's experience with a state system of unemployment insurance has been like that of other European countries. That is, during periods of abnormal unemployment, as in the depression years, the system is broken down by political pressure until it bears little if any resemblance to an actuarial insurance system. The machinery of the unemployment insurance scheme is made to serve for the distribution of government relief. Each of the Scandinavian countries, Professor Ratzlaff points out, has fully recognized the need for a three-fold coördinated program of cash payments, insurance benefits, and public works.

It is plain that the trade unions, with their high per-capita wealth, their large cash reserves, and their high wage level guaranteed by collective agreement, must have been an important factor in sustaining consumer purchasing power. And from this point of view labor's contribution to recovery looms large. Both employers and employees were, in certain respects, prepared to meet the emergency, with machinery long established to bring about necessary adjustments.

Because a sound foundation had been laid long ago for so many state and coöperative ventures, both social and economic, Sweden was prepared in other ways to meet the crisis. Thus the state, by virtue of the coördinated power block it has built up through the years, was in a position to electrify the state railroads, contributing a significant number of man-hours of work, both direct and indirect, to take up the slack left by the radical decline in private employment. The Coöperative Union, by reason of reserves carefully built up as a storm cellar for just such a contingency, was able to expand in a half dozen different directions at the very time that private capital was running for cover. The coöperative Luma plant was built during the depression. The coöperative Gislaved rubber factory was enlarged after the crisis had hit world trade. The Union built its handsome new office building at a time when private business was curtailing in every possible way. These projects were part of the Union's normal program of expansion but also they represent a shrewd move to take advantage of declining material costs. Because of the lucrative state monopolies, the government's revenues were less affected by the depression than in countries which depend entirely upon taxes.

If the coöperatives and the state industries are, as they seem to be, an effective check upon the growth of monopoly, then it is a fair assumption that these same forces served to temper the severity of the depression in Sweden. For they tended to prevent monopoly concentration of capital and industry and all the self-destructive elements inherent in the rapid concentration of wealth. This is, to be sure, an assumption, an imponderable. But it seems improbable that Sweden's extraordinary recovery is to be explained wholly by fortuitous circumstances without the borders of the country.

Nevertheless it is true that Sweden has been lucky. And while it would be less than justice to say that the Swedes have fished in the troubled waters of continental Europe, it is also true that many a prize catch has come to Sweden because of her very detachment, physical and political, from the European maelstrom. Thus with the Saar restored to Germany, industrialists in that area turned to Swedish iron ore, spurning the French whose wares they had previously been forced to accept. Luck, according to the old saw, comes only to those who are ready for it and Sweden even through the war and the difficult post-war adjustment has kept her economic house in order.

XII

DIRECTION FOR THE FUTURE

IF there had existed during the past two or three decades some sort of device for accurately measuring the decline of capitalism, the historian's task today would be enormously simplified. Some such thermometer for recording the temperature curve of a civilization would have been far more revealing than the crude measuring rods on which economists necessarily rely—indices of industrial production, of price levels, bank clearings, stock market activity, bankruptcies, and so on. The trend of capitalism toward monopoly, ever narrower and more restricted monopoly, and the significance of this trend would have been inescapably plain, perhaps even to capitalists themselves.

To be really worth while the curve would extend back almost to the eighteenth century and it would trace the rise of imperialism as an inevitable concomitant to industrial expansion. There would be certain parallels from country to country. The rapid advance of monopoly capitalism at the beginning of the present century was a phenomenon that was world-wide. But there would also be striking divergences.

At the point on the curve most strongly influenced by the monopoly trend Sweden would, I believe, show a marked divergence. In Sweden the significance of the mounting temperature, the hectic flush, was more or less clearly understood by the various doctors who claimed the right to direct the life of the state; or at least they did not disagree too violently. That is to say, the trend toward monopoly and the concentration of wealth was checked in various ways without a major conflict.

Sweden is almost the only country in the world in which capitalism has "worked" during recent decades. Checking the evolutionary development of capitalism at the point at which monopoly tends to distort the cycle of prosperity and depression, the Swedes seem to have interrupted the process of self-destruction which marked the economic life of other industrialized countries. In a sense it is the only country where *laissez faire* has continued to exist; where the so-called "laws" of supply and demand have not been wholly invalidated by the spread of monopoly. This may be further evidence, incidentally, of error in the early assumption that supply and demand worked in accord with the laws governing natural phenomena, quite apart from the complex activities of human beings in the modern world.

The degree of *laissez faire* that has continued to exist in Sweden is, in a manner of speaking, hothouse *laissez faire*. It exists under a bell-jar. The state, the consumer, and the producer have intervened to make capitalism "work" in a reasonable way for the greatest good of the whole nation. I have tried to show in what has gone before how this has been done: through state ownership and state competition; consumers' co-operation; producers' coöperation, and a strong, all-inclusive labor movement.

That this constitutes a fairly well-defined middle course seems to me obvious; it is a course between the absolute socialization of Russia and the end development of capitalism in America. In Russia, before the modifications introduced by Josef Stalin during the past four years, the rulers of the state attempted to make all of life conform to an idea, an ideal. In the United States the profit motive was put above every other consideration and it worked to the end of blind self-destruction.

The wisdom of the Swedes lies above all in their willingness to adjust, to compromise, to meet what appears to be reality. They have not been bound by a "system," nor have they been committed to a dogma. In a sense they are the ultimate pragmatists, interested only in the workability of the social order. This may explain why their contribution to political and social thought has been slight. Instead Sweden has offered the world a very salutary example of peace and well-being. If this has been achieved by adaptation and modification rather than by invention, it is none the less important.

Inasmuch as they are realists the Swedes have never persuaded themselves that all classes of society could benefit at the same time by social change. They have not hesitated to curtail or abolish profit, or the private businessman, when a desired change made this necessary. Thus the private wholesale trade in tobacco was abolished to furnish funds for starting the old-age pension system. It was a real gain to the workers, however small, for they were not made to pay for their own pensions out of wages.

Nor have the Swedes been persuaded of the possibility of regulating business in the interest of the public by law. There is nothing resembling an American anti-trust law on the statute books. The only law touching monopolies gives the state the right to investigate price-fixing by an enterprise "that can be considered to be of monopolistic nature." No attempt has been made at public utility regulation in the sense in which we use that word.

In their tax structure the Swedes show, too, that they are realists. Since 1910 there has existed a combined income and property tax. The latter is in effect a modest capital levy, equivalent to an annual assessment or income tax on one sixtieth of the declared net value of all property owned by the taxpayer at the end of the year. The base rate is not high, ranging up to 15 per cent on one million kronor and over. For example, an individual with a total taxable income of 20,000 kronor and property of a declared net value of 300,000 kronor would pay a tax on a total of 25,000; that is, one sixtieth of 300,000, which is 5,000, plus the 20,000 of income. The base rate applied to 25,000 kronor would be only 950 kronor.

Common Sense, a publication devoted to the interests of tax-payers, recently demonstrated that a man owning an estate assessed at a little over 2,000,000 kronor and receiving an income of 73,500 kronor, plus an earned income of 10,000 kronor, pays less than 30 per cent of his total tax on his income, whether earned or unearned, and 70 per cent on the estate itself. This amounts virtually to a capital levy.

But in 1934, to pay for the cost of the unemployment program, the government added 10 per cent to the base rate, making a total tax on this amount of 1,615 kronor; roughly an income and property tax of $400 assessed against an individual with a total taxable income of $5,000. In addition there is a municipal income tax and in many communities a municipal surtax on incomes above a certain level. The Stockholm rate for

1934 was 8.10 per cent and the municipal surtax in that year ranged from one half of a per cent up to 5 per cent.

The central government has consistently followed a pay-as-you-go tax policy. Rates were increased in proportion to increased spending. The result is that the cost of unemployment relief and the measures taken to check the effects of the depression will be paid for within five to six years. The budget for 1935–36 was balanced although the Swedes themselves do not lay undue stress upon this, holding it to be a matter of technical accountancy achieved as a matter of course within a reasonable governmental system.

The significance that Sweden's achievement may have for the world at large is debatable. It may be extremely limited. The state of peace, prosperity, and general well-being, in striking contrast to the disorder and unhealth in the rest of Europe, may come out of a national consciousness, a national pride, heightened by a realization of the dangers confronting a small country in imperialist-industrialist Europe. It may have merely a racial significance, a lesson in the value of certain neglected virtues— patience, perseverance, caution, with which the Swedes are particularly endowed. Certainly they have qualities which set them apart from most peoples. The Swedes are homogeneous to a remarkable degree. There is virtually no public graft in Sweden, a factor of primary importance if the state is to engage in large-scale enterprise. Social and economic education has penetrated to the mass of the people and it has been built upon an inherent regard for democratic institutions.

But when one has recited these and the other limitations which occur, there remains the fact that here is a country that has found for the time being at least a moderate solution for its problems. In a world torn by every sort of extreme this is not, even though the scale may be small, unimportant.

How long Sweden will be able to maintain the present balance depends obviously on such a number of factors that any prediction is worthless. It is a small state dependent upon world trade at a phase of rapid world change when one crisis follows upon another with almost monotonous regularity. It is, moreover, a capitalist country in which an owning class still exerts a considerable measure of control. One would scarcely predict the lengths to which this class, threatened with the loss of social and economic privileges, might go in its own defense.

At the depth of the depression troops were called out during a strike in the wood-pulp mills to the north. Firing upon the strikers, they killed two and wounded several. A wave of indignation swept the country, voiced not only by the Left but by the great majority of the Right. People were shocked and amazed. Such a thing could not happen in Sweden, they said, such a thing must not happen again.

One cannot forget the turn of events in Vienna. Every visitor to Europe who had any interest whatsoever in reform, housing, social progress, went as a matter of course to look at the magnificent workers' apartments that Vienna had built. But in a crisis, when the issue was essential power, the owning class did not hesitate to demolish those apartments by gunfire. This could never occur in Sweden, one is told. Our capitalists, say the Swedes, have been conditioned to yield, to compromise. And yet they have never been subjected to the test of a major crisis.

The Swedes put a high value upon democracy. Opposition to the totalitarian state, whether it be Fascist or Communist, is widely expressed. When Professor Gustav Cassel speaks of economic freedom and self-reliance and warns that "what stands to be lost is nothing less than the whole of that civilization that we have inherited from generations which once fought hard to lay its foundations and even gave their lives for it," he is not merely the mouthpiece of the owning class. Because economic freedom and a measure of independence have been preserved, through the state and the collective will of the consumer, it is probable that he speaks for a considerable portion of the public.

The Social-Democrats have no fixed, long-time program of socialization. They are committed to a cautious gradualism, advancing step by step with the approval of the overwhelming mass of the voters. Coming into office during the depression, they were faced with immediate problems of a most serious nature. It seemed for a time that they might have to take over certain industries that were on the verge of collapse. And they did not want to take over any industry in a dying condition. They preferred to bring about changes within their own time and by their own methods rather than under the pressure of a major emergency.

The Royal Commission on Socialization has been considering for more than ten years the trend toward socialism and the desirability of increasing or retarding the speed of the advance in that direction. The conservatives charge that the Social-Democrats have several times purposely delayed the report of the commission because the heads of the socialist party are not really in sympathy with socialization or because the commission has not succeeded in making a case for socialism. The Social-Democrats deny this. So long as the process of socialization could go forward quietly, without provoking violent controversy, they preferred not to raise the issue which publication of a report might have done.

They are concerned with the well-being of the social order rather than with socialization as a concept, as a goal. They would be less than human if they were not deeply gratified by the recovery that Sweden has achieved although they are frank to acknowledge that it may have come about in considerable part through external circumstances.

XIII

*SWEDEN REVISITED**

FROM the harbor the pattern of the city has a clear, bright simplicity. The red tile roofs, the fresh colors, the streets that give off from squares and parks, all these are well ordered to the eye. It is perhaps this orderly surface of Swedish life that first attracts the visitor who comes from a world in which violent extremes contend for power, in a civilization that must by comparison seem still amorphous. How far below the surface does this order extend? Does it approximate an inner harmony? Or does it conceal conflicts inevitably obscured from the visitor, however determined he may be to know the land and the people? These are questions that occur to one returning to Sweden after an interval of some years.

There is at present high prosperity in Sweden, with virtually no unemployment, and yet, through currency control, prices have been kept at a level more than 7 per cent under that of 1929. It is a prosperity that was well developed before the general European re-armament drive of 1936 gave to it the unnatural fillip of a boom. Undoubtedly, this prosperity contributed to the result of the election in September, 1936, when the Social-Democrats received much larger popular majorities than on the previous occasion, gaining eight additional representatives in the parliament. More important, as a result of this election the Social-Democrats for the first time formed an outright coalition government with the Farmers' party which also recorded popular gains; for four years they were allied with the Farmers, but the latter had not had executive responsibility.

The parliamentary position of the Labor-Farmer government is as strong as any in the history of the present system. During the past year this government has worked along two lines. First, it has sought to extend and enlarge present social services, at the same time developing new sources of revenue to meet these

* Reprinted by permission from the *Yale Review*.

added charges. Out of a sizable budgetary surplus, derived in large part from increased death duties imposed to meet the cost of public works during the depression, emergency loans are being rapidly repaid. A six-year period was assigned for the repayment of these emergency obligations.

Second, detailed plans are in preparation under this government for meeting a new economic crisis. In the event of another world depression, public funds are to be concentrated almost entirely on housing. The amount to be spent will, of course, be determined by the extent of unemployment, and the plans are therefore to be as flexible as possible. Working along this same line of heading off future trouble, the Minister of Foreign Affairs in the present Cabinet, R. J. Sandler, has taken the lead in bringing together Norway, Finland, Denmark, and Sweden for discussion of a system of joint neutrality and economic coöperation should a general European war occur. During the World War such a plan of neutrality was evolved only after hostilities had commenced and therefore under a great disadvantage. And the Prime Minister, Per Albin Hansson, has brought together the smaller powers included in the Oslo Convention to work for a revision downward of mutual tariff barriers. A gesture in the direction of freer trade, it may eventually produce tangible gains.

All this is in accord with the idea of progress in a democracy governed by representatives of the Labor-Farmer majority. In presenting this perspective on Swedish life, the outsider, the visitor, will almost certainly be guilty of oversimplification. How closely the social and political progress of the past twenty years has been dependent upon the skill, yes, the brilliance, with which Swedish industry has been organized, a visitor can scarcely say. Judgment on such a question must be left to the future historian of significant current phenomena.

There are many in Sweden today who deny the concept of progress under a Labor-Farmer government that seeks by orderly and lawful means to extend the benefits of machine civilization to the whole population. There is, first of all, a kind of red-faced arrogance among the more conservative which says that the present prosperity is its own creation and those who share in it do so at its tolerance. This attitude, which is rare.

denies that the government's expenditures for public works has had anything to do with recovery. The *Aftonbladet,* a Stockholm daily with a sensational "American" tone, owned by Torsten Kreuger, brother of the late Ivar, finds the concept merely "a pleasant social fiction." And this same newspaper makes a hero of Professor Bertil Ohlin, a Liberal economist, for having attempted in the course of a recent visit to America to correct the impression Americans have gained of Sweden as a fortunate land. It is Professor Ohlin who is trying to resuscitate the Liberal party, taking the lead in the "youth" movement of this "Folk-partiet."

From the middle-class, or a part of it, comes another sort of challenge to this concept of progressive democracy. Those who have thus far fallen outside the sphere of trade-union activity in Sweden often complain that the gains made by manual workers have been at the expense of the white-collar class. A correspondent who writes of the difficulties encountered in trying to organize office workers in a trade union has this to say: "The trade union man who has his automobile and maybe his motorboat, too, is not very much interested in people who are not in his class."

It is, however, those upon whom progress depends at the present moment, the leaders of the Social-Democratic party, who question most seriously and profoundly the concept of democracy—economic as well as political democracy. They are aware of the comparative ease with which a program of reform has been carried out in an expanding economy. Men like Ernst Wigforss, Minister of Finance, know how much more difficult the next steps will be; they realize at what an important phase the life of the Socialist party in Sweden has arrived.

For them it is not a little embarrassing that Sweden should be singled out in the present moment of world confusion and gloom as a "fortunate land." Aware as they are of how much remains to be achieved, in the face of obstacles certain to be graver than those encountered in the past, the present focus of interest on Sweden is disturbing to them. It is with an almost superstitious insistence, as one who fears to attract attention to his good fortune lest it change, that the members of the present Cabinet derogate their country's achievements to date.

There can be no doubt of the current interest of the outside world in Sweden as a "successful" social democracy. The number of American tourists has almost doubled in two years, and most of them have come to see the coöperative stores, the coöperative apartments, and other tangible evidences of social change. The more insistent and enthusiastic visitors have, indeed, created a serious problem for government officials and coöperative directors by making constant and impossible demands upon their time. As a result, it has been necessary to organize a "social tour," which takes in the more obvious points in Stockholm.

It is distressing to think that one may have contributed, however minutely, to the unceasing search of those Americans who still pursue around the world "the perfect little place"—where all the modern comforts can be found, and also a quaint picturesqueness that must be apparent to the least discriminating eye, setting the superior American definitely apart; and where, of course, everything can be got for nothing. Those who come to Sweden on such a search are disillusioned, and say so. "You can't find a comfortable bed in the entire country." "There simply isn't an adequate servant to be had if one goes outside Stockholm." "There's nothing to see, really nothing to see—it looks just like Wisconsin and Minnesota." "And it isn't cheap, no, not at all cheap." There is a great deal more tourist talk in this vein; about how unfeeling are the doctors, how inconsiderate the railway officials, how indifferent the hotelkeepers. No, Sweden is not that neat Utopia, complete with tiled showerbath and the most picturesque peasants, which many Americans have been seeking for so long.

As a matter of fact, the Swedes, with conspicuous exceptions, are not eager for the tourist trade. There is no certainty that this trade will continue, and to permit even a small fraction of the national economy to rest on so uncertain a base is to encourage trouble. Thus runs the reasoning of those who are concerned lest Sweden become another Switzerland. We cannot afford, they say, to build luxury hotels because our season is too short. And a great many Americans will be satisfied with nothing less than luxury hotels.

The English, too, are coming to Sweden in considerable numbers although, in general, with somewhat different demands. Yet here, also, a socio-economic interest has been a motive. In the summer of 1936 the New Fabian Research Bureau brought a party of students to Stockholm to observe conditions in a democracy governed by Socialists.

The Swedes are no more than human. There are those who would accept all this flattering attention at its face value. The discussion concerning the Swedish pavilion at the Paris Exposition brought that out. Certain members of the commission appointed to plan it favored a display which would show the country's very real social advance—evidence of the "middle way" that is so closely in accord with the Swedish temperament. But Professor Gunnar Myrdal, the brilliant young economist and a member of the parliament who has played an important part in the counsels of the Social-Democratic party, led a faction that took another point of view. Professor Myrdal said: "No, we cannot afford to do that; we can show the achievement, but it must be merely as the dynamic element by means of which we hope to raise standards which are still far too low." This was the line finally adopted by the commission.

Professor Myrdal tells a story that has circulated rather widely since the influx of American tourists. An American who had visited the coöperative apartments in Stockholm stopped a policeman in a working-class district and said, "This is all very well, this handsome city that I've been seeing, but I haven't seen your poor, where are your poor?" And the policeman replied: "Oh, sir, we are all poor but we don't talk about it." There is no little illumination of Swedish character in this, as there is in what Professor Myrdal himself has to say of the recent focus of interest in Sweden. It is one thing, he says, to single out the excellent phases of Swedish life; but this has inspired others who are determined to emphasize all the failures, if only to discredit the Socialists. And that, he adds, will be unfortunate for Sweden.

It seems to me evidence of the underlying vitality of this Northern democracy that the Swedes themselves have been able to bring national attention to bear on what is perhaps their most serious problem—the rapidly declining birth rate. The report of the Population Commission has revealed in a new and startling light the status of the underprivileged in the community. But even more important, if that is possible, it has transferred the issue of birth control and the question of human reproduction from the moral to the economic sphere. The size of families is seen to be related not so much to politics or morals as to income. And this report bears the signatures of twenty of the most eminent and respected leaders of the community— churchmen, public officials, scientists, and businessmen. It marks a fitting period to the ancient quarrel between Right and Left over birth control and sexual freedom, a quarrel that for many years has been merely the reflex of an old habit. Those who have taken an active part in the preparation of the report say, with justifiable pride, that it is doubtful whether in any other country such an objective statement of the relationship between human reproduction and the economics of the profit system could be issued under the names of nationally known leaders.

Based in considerable part on the population studies of Professor Myrdal and his wife, the report was intended to jar the complacency of flourishing, prosperous Sweden. And it has had just that effect. Many Swedes have been shocked by what has been disclosed about the people beyond the sphere of the prosperous two thirds, the world of the middle-class and the trade-union workers, the thriving industrial cities and towns.

In its most essential part the report is a revelation of the plight of a large share of the rural population, particularly in the North. The industrial revolution has left this section virtually unchanged, if anything lowering the standard of living. The small farmer in Norrland may have a cheap radio; but he has sent his cream and his butter into the world market to get it, and, as a result, his children may show definite signs of malnutrition. The report discloses, also, the very low cash incomes of the Northern farmers. Here, however, some observers feel that the picture has been made darker than the reality, not deliberately but because of the difficulty in getting at the real cash income of this farming population.

Even allowing for exaggeration, the rural picture is dark enough. The report shows that 44 per cent of all farm families receive an annual cash income of less than $250. The nutritional problem is directly related in the report to the size of farm incomes. It is shown that urban families with more than three children, on the lower income level, consume only about fifteen pounds of butter per person per year. But families with fewer children, or no children, on the same income level consume twice as much butter. And the same divergence is apparent in the consumption of other foodstuffs—milk, eggs, and vegetables. The report concludes that if families with three or more children consumed the average amount of these foodstuffs, the income of Swedish farmers would be increased by more than $25,000,000.

In the same way, the report relates the size of families to overcrowding in both city and country. Even in new apartment buildings there has been produced a standardized flat of one room, kitchen, and bath; and more than half of all the working-class families with more than three children live in this type of flat. Some Swedes seek to explain this by reference to the old peasant habit of sleeping in the kitchen because the kitchen was in the past the one warm room in the house. This habit, they say, has been carried over into modern life.

But the overcrowding that exists cannot be so easily explained away. The Population Commission reaches the startling conclusion that the improvement that has taken place in Swedish housing during the past twenty years has been due not so much to the provision of new apartment houses, many of them built with state aid, as to the birth of fewer children. In discussions of the report, opinions vary as to the reason for this overcrowding. Many are inclined to blame high labor costs in the building trades, the survival of what approximates a craft monopoly. Others blame ground rents.

On one point everyone with whom I have talked has been in agreement, and that is that, despite serious overcrowding, there are no slums in Sweden. And that, the Swedes say, is because we do not have the "slum mind." It is true that in the Swedish character there is a deeply rooted love of order and cleanliness and with this goes a desire to present the best possible appearance to the world. It is this last trait, the report of the commission concludes, which presents a problem more or less apart from economic reform. The middle class is determined upon a standard of comfort and leisure incompatible with children and family life. This class must be made to realize that the well-being of the nation depends upon the family.

Fewer than 5 per cent of all families in Stockholm have three children or more, and less than 12 per cent of all families in the capital have two children. The present Swedish birth rate, the report makes clear, is nearly 30 per cent below the level required to maintain merely a stationary population. At present, about half of all Swedish households have one child or none, and it will be necessary for at least half of this number to have a minimum of four children if the population is to remain stationary.

While the Swedish birth rate is declining more rapidly than that of almost any other nation, Sweden is not the only country in the Western world that is disturbed by this vital problem of a dwindling population. The Swedes are thus far, however, the only people to face the facts with intelligence and without shrinking from any of the implications. In Germany and Italy the dictators invoke offspring with a primitive emotionalism; people must breed in order that there shall be soldiers to die for the glory of the Fatherland. That children shall be born into a world of violence and despair is, of course, quite incidental. And one thinks, too, of the enormous abyss between wealth and poverty in Great Britain, an abyss that is more and more taken for granted.

Nor is it possible to ignore the mote in the American eye; those comforting fictions about an "American living standard" which so conveniently overlook vast areas, the South, the Appalachian Highlands, the Ozarks, the "dust bowl." Counting the number of automobiles per capita, all too often we disregard statistics on the consumption of essential foodstuffs. Why not a Population Commission for America?

During the last four years Sweden, despite financial and cultural ties of long standing, has turned away from Germany and at the same time has drawn closer to Great Britain. Just now the government is fostering closer relations with Russia. As one move in that direction Aerotransport, the state-controlled air line, has opened a new air route which makes it possible to fly from London to Moscow in something less than ten hours, with a stop-over at Stockholm, providing a dramatic series of contrasts. Mr. Sandler has been in Moscow on a kind of good-will excursion, and the Stockholm newspapers have had many pictures of him with Mr. Litvinoff and with Madame Kollantai, who is the Russian Minister to Sweden.

Toward the Spanish government in its struggle with the Moorish-German-Italian forces of General Franco a large part of the Swedish public has shown deep sympathy. Swedish trade unionists say that Sweden has sent more money, proportionately, to the Spanish Loyalists than any other nation in the world, a large part of it, of course, from trade-union sources. In the remote northern town of Kiruna members of the miners' union recently voted to give a day's pay to the Loyalists, sending out to Madrid a draft for $2,000, which was in addition to more than $5,000 previously sent from this town of less than ten thousand population. Most of the important newspapers have, with varying degrees of enthusiasm, taken the Loyalists' side of the controversy. Stress has been placed on the struggle of democracy to survive the aggressions of dictatorship.

The suggestion that a similar conflict may take place in the Scandinavian peninsula is received with open incredulity. I have not talked to any responsible person who believes that there is a possibility of either Fascism or Communism in Sweden. The nearest hint of an extreme attitude came from a capitalist who expressed the "fear" that the Socialists would go "too far" and create an inevitable reaction, perhaps on the pattern of German Naziism. And that fear may have been more nearly a hope. This is not to say that there is any certainty whatsoever as to what might or might not happen in the event of another European war, waged with far less regard for neutral powers than the last one. Should Europe be swept by a wave of Fascism or Communism following such a conflict, there is no one so optimistic as to believe that the Scandinavian peninsula would be isolated from the general contagion.

On the extreme Left, there are now three small Communist factions instead of two as before; and the largest group is seeking, in accord with the "new line" out of Russia, to make a common front with the Socialist majority. For their part, the

Socialists, who had learned to expect sharp opposition from this quarter, do not take the effort too seriously.

Coming from London or Paris to Stockholm, one cannot but sense a marked difference in the emotional climate. There is not the same preoccupation with the Spanish conflict, nor is there the omnipresent dread of a debacle that in London is as real a thing as the Nelson Column in Trafalgar Square. The Swedes go about the job in hand relatively free from the haunting fear that in so much of Europe makes every gesture appear futile; the weary reflex of a mechanism that is plunging toward destruction.

The Swedish Coöperative Union has taken several important steps in the last four years. There has been considerable expansion in Stockholm, both in the central offices of the Union and in the large department store that was acquired in 1934. Recently the Union bought a large porcelain plant, and serious consideration is being given to expanding it in such a way— "rationalizing" it, as a favorite Swedish expression goes—that large-scale production of plumbing fixtures will be possible. This, with the price reduction that coöperators are confident they can achieve, will be a real contribution to the housing problem. Swedish coöperators through their Coöperative Union have entered into a partnership with the Scottish Wholesale Coöperative Society by way of British Luma, a company formed in Glasgow for the manufacture of electric light bulbs. The Scandinavian Luma and British Luma will share the services of a technical director, in accordance with an extremely interesting and significant agreement.

Among middle-class critics there are ironic references to the Coöperative Union as "Sweden's greatest trust." But Albin Johansson and the other directors are undisturbed by this kind of criticism. Mr. Johansson is hammering away at the line he has always followed—distribution of an ever greater volume of goods through lower and lower prices. The Coöperative Union has recently sought to impress this point of view on the farmers' producer coöperatives, which have been largely instrumental in obtaining from the government subsidies that are the equivalent of price guarantees. Mr. Johansson does simple arithmetic in his deliberate, careful way, showing how many thousand pounds of butter were sold in Stockholm when the price was at one level and how much less was sold when the price was raised. It is through such obvious demonstrations that he preaches his philosophy of lower prices and wider distribution.

The state power system has been expanding at a rate far in advance of that laid down in the long-time program. Yet, according to W. Borgquist, director of the Royal Board of Waterfalls, it can scarcely meet the demands made upon it. Similarly rapid progress is being made in the electrification of the state railways.

And, most important of all, practical immediate plans are being considered to correct the serious defects disclosed by the report of the Population Commission. Social-Democratic leaders are studying the possibility of revising the entire agricultural program of the government. Sweden, they say, has been dumping her "surplus" agricultural produce onto the world market at the world price at the same time that the government has been sustaining a higher domestic price. It is time to stop that. This so-called "surplus," which the report of the Population Commission has shown to be no surplus at all, must be made available to Sweden's own people who need it. The money to pay for it? From a higher income tax perhaps. Somehow the money must be found, since this is not a question of political theory but of children who need essential foodstuffs. It will be easy enough to find ways to distribute this "surplus" food; free lunches to all school children, unlimited quantities of free milk in all schools, the cost to be paid by the central government.

Recently a hundred and seventy members of the parliament made an exhaustive and, so they said, exhausting tour of Norrland to observe the conditions that the Population Commission had reported upon. They will have first-hand information to use in the debate on this vital question which will undoubtedly be opened shortly after the parliament meets again.

Yes, here each man has his job, and he works at it, seriously and conscientiously. One recalls recently published letters in which the late Justice Holmes remarked that if a man did his work six days a week, the seventh day was his to do what he liked with, for he had fulfilled his duty to mankind. It comes back, perhaps, to the business of character. Again and again, as in the past, I have been impressed by what it means to be one people with an ancient tradition and certain shared qualities: of jealous pride that engenders, on the one hand, a deeply rooted independence and self-respect and, on the other, stubborn stoicism and impassivity; of caution and deliberation. This time I have been made particularly aware of two manifestations of Swedish character. The first is an underlying sense of justice which seems to be a real factor in many relationships. And the other is a regard for the well-being of the land—for the natural balance of air, earth, and water plus people dependent upon these elements, which in Sweden takes so many interesting forms.

To the well-ordered pattern that one perceives on the surface of life certain traditions contribute, traditions which America has not known. One, of course, is the class system. While the Swedes themselves differ as to how operative in their country this system now is, there is no doubt that it is a powerful survival out of the past. It is certainly not as rigid as Britain's caste system, enforced by means of the public school taboo. But just as certainly it is a reality even though today people, or, at least, superior people, pass from class to class with comparative ease.

In any discussion of Europe, such survivals must be taken for granted; behavior patterns left more or less intact despite the upheavals of the past century and a half. But with due allowance for this inheritance, I feel that the essential order, the health, of this people strikes well below the surface; that a kind of balance between past and present has been achieved. I put this down, with all humility, as the impression of a visitor, a reporter, returning to Sweden for the third time.

Here where I am writing, at the Tourist Station at Riksgränsen, on the extreme northern boundary of the country, almost a hundred miles within the polar circle, one is made aware of how well the Swedes have organized their world. The snow-capped granite mountains that look off to Norway—old Norway—are grand and wild and lonely. From the mountaintops there is no desecrating sign of man. But at this inn, which exists principally for skiers in the spring, there are the modern creature comforts in an atmosphere of pleasant, simple charm; it is well organized and well run. The power lines and the long-distance telephone wires run off across the mountains—the great world is very close.

From the top of the granite cliff before the inn the view is out to distant snows that appear to have been undisturbed since the glacier passed. Looking down there is an infinitesimal electric train pulling a long line of ore cars up the steep grade to Narvik; iron ore from the mines of Kiruna which is two hours to the south. Kiruna, the mines, the town itself, that is a larger example of organization under difficulty. The ore is bound for Germany and Britain. It will go into armaments.

Even here in this remote place one is confronted with the lunatic base on which the economic structure of all Europe is now resting. When it falls, from war or whatever impetus, will any remnant of sanity survive anywhere in the world? If the structure of this society—the framework within which reasonable changes have thus far been brought about—is threatened, will any moderation prevail? There is no answer in the present to questions of this kind. Meanwhile the Swedes are doing the job that is before them.

XIV

POSTWAR SWEDEN

THE world has undergone devastating changes in the decade since this book was first published. A war more terrible than any other in history has swept the entire globe. Great cities have been reduced to rubble. Powerful nations have been brought low. Whole peoples have reverted to a barbarism that is more terrifying because it wields the weapons of modern science. The very frame of European life has been threatened with utter breakdown.

Yet Sweden has come through this holocaust seemingly untouched. This, of course, is merely the surface impression. Even though the Swedes escaped German occupation by a narrow margin, they have been subjected to the destructive, disruptive forces unleashed by the war. They have felt the strong pressure of inflation. They have suffered severely from the lack of such vital commodities as oil and coal. They have seen the trend toward urbanization and greater centralization which is a universal effect of modern war. Geographical boundaries could not keep out the disruptive moral and emotional currents that stemmed from the Nazi revolution and the war that followed it.

Nevertheless the fact that Sweden is still a democracy, relatively sound and whole, and still determined to try to follow a "middle way" is in itself a kind of miracle. The reasons why Sweden escaped occupation, and therefore the most disastrous effects of the war, are many and complicated. That is a story which can be told only when the documents and the memoirs are available. Because of the part played by Soviet Russia, and particularly by that remarkable woman, Madame Alexandra Kollontai, who was Soviet Minister to Stockholm during the war, the true story may never be told. Russian secrecy may keep back too many essential details.

Both good luck and good management had a part. Those Swedes who were nearest the storm center say that luck was the more important element. Several days before the invasion of

Norway and Denmark in 1940, the Swedish intelligence service had fairly complete information on the Nazis' plans. This was passed on to the foreign ministers of both countries. But so strong was the habit of neutrality that they could not bring themselves to believe it, especially in the face of earnest denials from Berlin.

The Danes and the Norwegians, the latter in particular, know at bottom that it was to their advantage that Sweden remained neutral and unoccupied. Fifty-thousand Norwegians escaped over the border to freedom and nearly six thousand reached England to take part in the fight. Similarly, thousands of Danes passed back and forth, part of the underground working incessantly to undermine the German occupation. The contribution that Sweden made, quietly and covertly, to the Allied victory was considerable. Secretly Sweden provided scarce war materials which were flown out in Allied planes. More important was the intelligence which came out through Swedish channels. Since the war the Swedes have told a large part of this story, perhaps more than they should have told since it advertised the fact that their neutrality was a carefully designed façade. If anything like neutrality is possible in a future war, the Swedes may have cause to regret their frankness. At the same time the Swedes were bitterly attacked for continuing to send to Germany such essentials as ball bearings. There were times when it was almost impossible to maintain the position of a neutral.

It is hard to forgive your neighbor both good luck and good management. As Sweden persisted in her cautious course of neutrality during the long and terrible years of the war, a deep resentment grew up among the occupied peoples of Norway and Denmark. That was intensified when, following rumors widely published in Sweden, the Swedes failed to move into Norway and Denmark in the closing weeks of the war to prevent the final carnival of murder and destruction that everyone had feared would mark the Nazi Götterdämmerung.

This resentment is a very real factor today. It gets in the way of the kind of coöperation which could weld the Scandinavian countries into a single, unified whole; a unit that would keep the flags, the symbols, the traditions but would abolish the folly of customs, the top-heavy bureaucracy of nationalism. That is beginning to happen but it is a slow process.

Sweden wants first of all to coöperate with her neighbors in a kind of federation such as sovereign states have never before achieved. Working with her neighbors, she wants to be part of the United Nations. Here, of course, there are deep reservations and doubts. In the 'twenties the League of Nations had no more passionate and loyal support than that which came from the Scandinavian Peninsula. The failure and the dissolution of the League were the source of great sorrow and disillusionment in Sweden.

The fear in Sweden, as in other small nations, is that the UN has within it the same seeds of dissolution. Yet, as a small nation in a world dominated by two or three great powers, the Swedes have no recourse but to work through the new organization.

The position of the small nation was perilous before World War II. That position is even more perilous today. Sweden has important deposits of uranium. How important those deposits are is a state secret, although geologists have in general a fairly good idea of how rich the prize is. It is as though one of the smallest boys in school had a priceless agate. The Swedes know they have a dangerous possession.

If the Scandinavian states can achieve coöperation that is more than a mere form, here is an opportunity to demonstrate to the world what the peacetime uses of atomic energy can mean. Let the three countries go together to construct an atomic energy plant. If some such plan could be worked out, it should surely be possible to entrust these three peaceful peoples with technical information and with the machines which they could not make themselves.

Just here, of course, you come up against the fear of Soviet Russia. It is a fear which in Sweden has deeper roots than elsewhere. Through the fifteenth and sixteenth centuries Russia was the traditional enemy. Russia was a semibarbaric country and the Swedes prided themselves on their civilization. The Mongol invader from the steppes was partly a fearful legend and partly a real threat.

The passionate support of Finland during the Russo-Finnish war of 1939–40 owed not a little to this legendary fear. It also had a practical base in the fact that Finland is less than half an hour away by air. Russia across the Baltic had a somewhat different look, even in the air age, than Russia next door.

This is the present reality. While it has thus far been a relatively mild domination, the fact remains that Finland today is under the thumb of the USSR. With minor exceptions, Finnish policy is determined by what Moscow does.

The Swedes are above all realists. They recognize the power that Soviet Russia exerts in the world today. They understand that they cannot permit their emotions to dominate when they live next door to one of the two greatest powers in the world. This is the real explanation for Sweden's Russian policy.

There are other reasons, too. Before the war approximately 20 per cent of Sweden's trade was with Germany. Germany provided nearly one fifth of Sweden's coal. Now Germany is a ruin with a dubious future. Sweden must get oil and other raw materials and she must have an outlet for the machines she manufactures.

The $250,000,000 Swedish trade agreement with Russia has political as well as economic aspects. It does no good to deny that, as the Minister of Commerce, Gunnar Myrdahl, did in an interview with American journalists in the fall of 1946. The existence of the Soviet power on Sweden's border is a geographical and political fact of overwhelming importance. The agreement is a recognition of that reality.

It is beset with perils. The Swedes know that better than anyone else. They realize that they are playing with economic fire. But even if they had wanted to follow another course, it is extremely doubtful that an alternative existed.

Inside Sweden much of the debate turned on how extensive a credit should be advanced to Russia. The Labor government argued that if generous credits were advanced to other countries —and they were advanced—then credits on a similar scale would have to be granted to the USSR. To insist on less generous terms would be to imply a suspicion that could be regarded as unneighborly. Such an attitude would hardly be wise for little Sweden. In their new and burgeoning power the Russians are extremely sensitive.

Some critics of the agreement have serious doubts as to the volume of raw materials which Sweden will receive during the five-year term. They are skeptical about Russian promises to deliver oil. They are fearful that the exchange will be hopelessly lopsided, with repayment only a distant mirage that the great power can dismiss with contempt. The most deep-seated fear, of course, is that the agreement ties Sweden's economy too closely to the Communist colossus. It covers up to 20 per cent of Sweden's export trade, which is a sizable proportion.

There are still other doubts on the score of whether Swedish industrialists can deliver the machines the Russians want in the volume that they want them. During the negotiations leading up to the trade agreement, the Russians repeatedly failed to specify the kind and the quantity of manufactures that they wanted. When they finally supplied the lists, they were told that because of the delays the volume of goods would inevitably be smaller. Swedish industrialists had in the meantime made commitments to customers in other countries.

This last the Russians found very difficult to understand. They could scarcely comprehend a government which could not order its citizens to obey simple directions about production quotas. Sometimes they took a high-handed attitude with the industrialists, not placing orders but giving orders. This has given rise to no little trepidation. A group of conservative businessmen complained that under the agreement the Soviets would have two hundred agents inside Sweden supervising the carrying out of individual contracts.

The most serious objections have come from the Liberals. They have not hesitated to speak out against the shadow of totalitarianism. These same Liberals were in many instances those who spoke out boldly against the Nazi tyranny. They recognize the threat to all freedom in the spread of Communism and in the subtle persuasion that safety and security lie in alliance with the USSR. Herbert Tingsten, a professor of political economy who was made editor of *Dagens Nyheter,* the nation's leading newspaper, has written fearlessly and brilliantly of the threat to a free society that he believes to be inherent in the Russian agreement.

Opposition came also from Professor Bertil Ohlin, head of the Liberal party. As Minister of Commerce in Sweden's wartime coalition government, Professor Ohlin first proposed a loan agreement with Soviet Russia. After the coalition government was dissolved with the end of the war, Ohlin based his objections to the agreement on the size of the credits it was proposed to grant to the Soviets.

The fact that Liberals in Sweden opposed the agreement with Communist Russia does not mean that they are persuaded of the perfection of capitalism. Professor Ohlin, and others who think as he does, have decided reservations about American capitalism at any rate. While they do not take as gloomy a view as Myrdahl, who predicted an inevitable crash following the war, they have serious reservations about our stability. They are skeptical, too, on the score of our government of divided powers. They wonder whether the Federal government in Washington could move quickly enough to avert a depression.

The political tag of liberal means something rather different in Sweden than it does in the United States, where more often than not it is appropriated either by those who subscribe to a complete *laissez faire* Adam Smith viewpoint or by fellow travelers on the Communist line. As the leader of his party, Professor Ohlin subscribes to the entire social security program that has been put into effect during the past twenty-five years. He believes in raising social security rates. He believes in expanding and improving a system of public medicine which makes low cost medical care possible for every social class.

Where the Liberal differs from the Social-Democrat is on the question of nationalization. With the end of the war and the formation of a Socialist government, the Socialists proposed to nationalize the oil industry, insurance, and the manufacture of shoes. These proposals were advanced tentatively. Royal commissions were put to work to recommend the proper steps to carry out this program.

How seriously the government intended these proposals to be taken is a question. The Minister of Finance, Ernst Wigforss, is a strong advocate of nationalization. He has some followers in the Socialist party. But during the municipal election campaign in the fall of 1946, the Labor party deliberately soft-pedaled the issue of nationalization. The Liberal party made much of it, which may have been the reason the Liberals gained more than any other party.

By standards outside Sweden the changes registered in the election were very small. The Liberal party went from just under 13 per cent of the total vote, at the last preceding election, to 15½ per cent. The Communists gained less than had been expected, going from 10 to 11 per cent of the total. In power for fourteen years, with one minor interlude excepted, the Social-Democratic party polled nearly 45 per cent, which is 2 per cent above the vote the party received when the Social-Democrats first came into office. The Conservatives suffered the heaviest losses, which was quite understandable since the members of their party are dying off and are not being replaced by a younger generation.

The Communist campaign approach was exactly that which Communists have taken all over the world. Their campaign posters demanded, with eloquent simplicity, lower prices and higher wages. Their strategy was to exploit the troubles of the government, which was just then seeking to hold down rapidly mounting prices so that a new mandatory cost-of-living wage increase would not have to be granted. Naturally, therefore, the Communists agitated for higher wages.

Their position in this respect, however, was somewhat weakened by what had occurred shortly after the end of the war. The metal fabricators union, in which the Communists had considerable influence, went on strike for a wage that was regarded by employers in the industry as exorbitant. The strike lasted for five months. It cost the union several hundred thousand dollars in strike benefits. Finally it was settled on the basis of the offer which the companies had originally made. This did not enhance the prestige of the Left wing within the labor movement.

In the controversy over nationalization the stand taken by the coöperatives, under the leadership of Albin Johansson, is extremely interesting. Increasingly in recent years Johansson has become concerned over the world-wide trend toward state control over trade. He believes passionately in a free economy as the best means of getting lower costs and higher quality. At the same time, of course, he recognizes that if consumers do not act in their own interest, the end result will almost certainly be either state control or private monopoly; hence the coöperative movement in which Johansson has played such a prominent part. Believing in a free economy, Johansson started out in a characteristically practical way to checkmate the move toward nationalization in Sweden.

He began with an attack on the proposal to nationalize the oil industry. What he did was to persuade organizations whose members are the principal consumers of petroleum products in the country to band together with the coöperative societies. In the end this league against nationalization included a very large segment of the voting population. It was far too powerful a group to alienate and that is one reason why the Socialists played down nationalization as an election issue.

Eventually the government may build a large oil refinery. Johansson and his fellow coöperators would not oppose it. Such a refinery, if run as efficiently as similar enterprises have been run under state ownership, would provide a yardstick of competition. It would be a yardstick both for private business and for the coöperatives. As Swedish coöperators see it, competition today must take place not so much between individuals as between elements in the economy, since centralization and monopoly have advanced so far already. For this reason all conscientious liberals must work hard to promote the kind of competition which will keep the economy at least relatively free.

Within the coöperative movement, and stemming particularly from Johansson, is strong support for the kind of world-trade organization which has been projected by the United States. The Swedes, who are preëminently realists, believe that active, positive steps must be taken if we are to get anything like free trade in the world again. Outworn restrictions on private trade such as tariffs must be abolished. Otherwise, in his view, the Western world will never be able to compete with Russia. As the Russian glacier moves, it cuts down geographical barriers. Whether through mutually exclusive trade treaties, as in the Balkans, or through direct annexation, as in the Baltic States, the Soviet Union frees the way for an exchange of goods; the only trade restrictions existing are those that keep out every other nation.

A strong Swedish delegation went to Zurich for the first international congress of the coöperative movement since 1937. Held in the fall of 1946, the congress had originally been scheduled for 1942. The Swedish coöperators gave support to the proposal for an international oil coöperative. The plan for such a coöperative—a bold and venturesome undertaking to say the least—was worked out by a special committee. A member of that committee is Howard Cowden of Kansas City who has had an important part in developing the coöperative refining and wholesaling of petroleum products for distribution to retail coöperatives throughout the United States. Johansson met Cowden in the course of a tour of the United States. They are both keenly interested in getting the new international coöperative started.

At the congress in Zurich the Russian delegation opposed the plan. Reluctantly British and Scottish coöperatives approved it. They hesitated because of their existing relationships with large private oil suppliers. Without the support of British and Scots, of course, the plan could never be realized. If the vast coöperative market in Great Britain can be supplied by an international co-op, then it would seem to have a good chance of success. It would be something new under the sun, a David challenging the Goliaths of the international petroleum trade with all its ramifications in high politics. One thing could be expected and that is that the giants would fight it in every possible way.

The war somewhat checked the expansion of the coöperatives in Sweden. With rising prices, however, the membership has increased until today the coöperative movement enrolls well over one third of all consumers. Plans are being pushed for expansion of the porcelain works at Gustavsberg to manufacture low-cost plumbing fixtures in large volume. The high cost of the things that go into a house is a factor, as elsewhere in the world, in Sweden's very severe housing shortage.

Under the direction of Johansson and the men around him the coöperatives have been preëminently successful. Leading co-operators participate in every phase of Swedish life. They were among the businessmen who took part in the negotiations with Soviet Russia in Moscow.

But in recent years participation by the rank and file of the membership has not matched the record of successful operation. There has been a definite falling away of interest on the part of the average citizen who belongs to a coöperative because it means a saving on his household bills. This is a source of deep concern to many within the coöperative movement.

It is the subject of searching self-criticism by coöperators themselves. Because the men at the top are so able, the natural tendency is to permit them to make the vital decisions. The skill of the managers leaves little room for the democratic process. This is contrary to coöperative theory and belief. But it is what is happening in actual practice and those whose beliefs are rooted in the high idealism of the movement worry about ways and means to reverse the tendency.

Somewhat the same thing is happening in the political life of the country. It may, of course, be no more than the enormous disruption of the war with the fierce currents of hope and fear and suspense that were set in motion in Sweden as everywhere. Reason was obscured. The coalition government during the war submerged all political differences. On the whole this government worked with remarkable harmony, but during that interval the political consciousness of the people was suspended.

With the end of the war it was not easy to recapture the old partisanship which provoked debate and challenge that in turn held public attention. After the blood and thunder of the dictators the politics of reason seem tame and flat. Not that any more than a small fringe, and for the most part a lunatic fringe, was ever attracted in Sweden to the Fascist extreme. But the drama of Germany, with all its terror and horror, made a deep impression on a people who had lived for so long as neighbors to the Germans.

A great gap was left in Sweden's political life with the death of Prime Minister Per Albin Hansson at the age of sixty. He died, as he lived, with the utmost simplicity. On his way to his suburban home on a streetcar at the end of a long conference on the Russian agreement, he died because his heart stopped beating. He was a great man. What he did for Sweden will be apparent only with the passage of the years.

Per Albin had come to be a symbol of the middle way. In his deliberateness, his calmness, his refusal to be stampeded, he was the essence of reasonable compromise which in turn is the essence of Sweden's successful adjustment to the age of technology. I have rarely met any public figure who was so genuinely self-effacing. While he took his job with intense seriousness, he did not take himself with the deadly self-righteousness that too often stamps public men as vainglorious egotists. When he was asked about the stresses and strains of the war, he always laughingly protested that he was never troubled by decisions once they were made and that he slept well and soundly no matter what the tensions of the day.

It is probable, however, that the war took a greater toll than he realized or than he cared to admit. Harrowing issues had to be met. In the last analysis it was the Prime Minister who had to decide whether German troops on leave should be allowed to cross the country from Norway to Finland and later from Norway down into Germany and back. And when the decision was taken, he had to defend it. While from inside the government it may have seemed an inevitable decision, there were many to denounce it. The late Torny Segerstedt, editor of the *Göteborg Handelstidningen*, was a fiery crusader for the Allies, repeatedly denouncing the government for its caution and timidity.

There was never any doubt where the sympathies of Per Albin and the members of the government lay. They hated the Nazis just as much as Segerstedt. But they were faced with a reality. If Sweden had resisted the German demand for transit of leave troops, for example, one of several things might have happened. At the very least the Germans could have cut off all or most of the coal essential to sustain Swedish industry. So far as actual invasion was concerned, the Swedes were determined to make the Nazis pay as dearly as possible. Throughout the war Sweden kept several hundred thousand men under arms. In late January of 1942 the full strength of the Swedish Army was mobilized on the frontiers in response to intelligence that set the date for a Nazi invasion of the country. After the Swedish mobilization, Hitler is said to have decided that he could not spare the necessary extra German divisions from the Russian front. Swedish resistance would eventually have been overcome but it would have been costly to the Germans.

Throughout the war hundreds of refugees found their way to Sweden. This was an objective that Per Albin Hansson worked toward always. Many were Jews from Europe who would otherwise have gone into the death furnaces. If the United States had admitted refugees in the same proportion, we would have taken in 1,600,000 persons. Actually during the same period fewer than a thousand refugees were admitted to this country.

In some respects the death of Per Albin is comparable to the loss of Franklin Roosevelt. The span of office of the two men covered very nearly the same period. Both embodied for many people the political idealism and social objectives of a transition period. As Roosevelt dominated the Democratic party, so, in a sense, did Hansson dominate the Social-Democratic party in Sweden.

But the domination by the American President was far more nearly a matter of personal prestige and power. Per Albin was the leader of a team; the men on that team had come up with him through the discipline of a closely integrated political party. As members of Parliament, they were accustomed to working together in close coöperation within the framework of a government both responsive and responsible. There is nothing like the division of powers that exists under the American system, which seems to call forth personal intrigue and personal rivalry.

While Sweden suffered materially during the war, as for example in the inroads made in the forest reserves because of the critical lack of coal, she also used the interval to good advantage. Swedish shipyards turned out a number of modern freight-passenger vessels that are now competing for world trade. When the war ended Swedish industrialists had a running head start toward full production in supplying the desperate demand of nearly every European country. In spite of the pinch of high prices, the country has a prosperous look. There is a serious shortage of manpower which may be met by encouraging immigration. The shortage of housing in the cities, and particularly in Stockholm, is as acute as anywhere in the world. One consequence is the pitiful advertisements in which people in desperation appeal for a basement room or a garret. Rationing of scarce foods continued through 1946, although the rations were relatively generous.

The visitor to Sweden who has seen the rest of Europe in ruins feels as though he were entering a living museum in which not only the monuments but the values of the past have been miraculously preserved. It is enormously heartening to find men with alert minds discussing the issue of freedom versus totalitarianism and discussing it with vigor and courage. Moreover, they are aware of the present; they do not talk in terms of an impossible retreat to the *laissez-faire* world of the eighteenth century.

Beneath the surface of well-being are the doubts which trouble all of mankind. More than ever before the realization has struck home that the future depends on some sort of international accord. No amount of good fortune and good management can possibly save a small country if the great powers go to war again. The weapons of the new warfare are such that even the fiction of neutrality will no longer exist. The atomic bomb has ended once and for all the old concept of sovereign nations electing or not electing to go to war. Informed Swedes understand that the future lies within the United States of America and the United States of Soviet Russia. That is why they look from east to west and back again.

But this realization has not deterred them from following their own course of development. It has not blunted their national consciousness in which pride of achievement is such an important factor. Their belief in a middle way has if anything been strengthened by what has happened during the past decade. They have seen absolutisms perish and go down. So they continue on the course of conscience, of patience, of painstaking compromise that looks to human satisfaction.

INDEX

THE YALE PAPERBOUNDS

Now in the Yale Paperbound series

THE YALE SHAKESPEARE